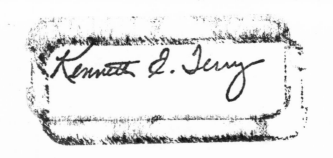

Audiovisual Media in
Christian Education

Audio-Visual media

IN CHRISTIAN EDUCATION

by

GENE A. GETZ

MOODY PRESS • CHICAGO

© 1972 by
THE MOODY BIBLE INSTITUTE
OF CHICAGO

A complete revision of the earlier
Audio-Visuals in the Church

Library of Congress Catalog Card Number: 73-181587

ISBN: 0-8024-0365-4

Fifth Printing, 1977

Printed in the United States of America

Contents

Illustrations

Acknowledgments

The author wishes to express sincere appreciation to the following people and organizations for advice, counsel, materials, ideas and visuals which have assisted greatly in making this revised edition of *Audiovisual Media in Christian Education* a reality:

Joel A. Benedict
Miss Vivienne Blomquist
Joe E. Buresch
Richard Focht
Dr. Harold Garner
Loren Getz
Dave Harbough
Dr. Howard Hendricks
Phil Lasse
Dr. Lois LeBar
Duane Litfin
Mrs. Keïth Miller
Don Regier
Grosvenor Rust
Clarence Spencer
AKAI Company
American Optical Corporation
Barnett and Jaffe
Bell and Howell Company
Buhl Optical Company
Charles Beseler Company
Christian Life Magazine
Da-Lite Screen Company
Dallas Theological Seminary
Dukane Corporation

Eastman Kodak Company
Educational Technology
Gospel Recordings, Inc.
H. Wilson Company
Infronics Company
Minnesota Mining and Manufacturing Company
Montage Company
Moody Monthly Magazine
Moody Press
Norelco
Polaroid
Projection Optics Co.
Rheem Califone
Seal Inc.
Scripture Press Publications
Singer Society for Visual Education, Inc.
Sony Corporation of America
Standard Publishing Company
Standard Projection Company
Teach Magazine, Gospel Light Publications
Technifax Corporation
Viewlex

Foreword

WITHOUT QUESTION the first edition of Dr. Getz's book on audiovisuals has greatly influenced teaching methods and the use of teaching tools in the local church. *Audio Visuals in the Church* was the first in-depth treatment of this subject published by an evangelical press. In the dozen years since, thousands of students in Bible institutes, Christian colleges and seminaries have studied it as a standard text in courses in teaching techniques and audiovisual communications. The principles, methods and knowledge of audiovisual teaching tools have in turn been taught to Christian education leaders and teachers in the local church, who have been encouraged in their work as they have learned how to use media in communicating the Word.

The double entrance to the mind through both the eye-gate and ear-gate has helped teachers to make truth crystal clear, to keep learning interesting, and to build bridges between themselves and their students, and between the known and the unknown. "The hearing ear, and the seeing eye, the LORD hath made even both of them" (Pr 20:12).

This revised edition is an outgrowth of additional research, continued observation, a keen awareness of current trends in Christian education, and of personal use. In spite of a grueling schedule, Dr. Getz has taken time to keep abreast of educational developments in both the secular and the Christian education fields. His contributions have been monumental and have been widely accepted and fully appreciated throughout this country as well as abroad. His numerous books, his teaching ministry on both the Bible-institute and seminary level, his success as an administrator, his response to demands as a Christian education consultant and conference speaker, and his personal practical involvement in Christian education on the local church level have helped establish him as an outstanding authority in the field of Christian education. He has distinguished himself as thorough in his research, lucid in his writing, and practical in his application.

The dynamic of Dr. Getz's work has been his continuing recognition of the ministry of the Holy Spirit, for it is "not by might of excellent methods, nor by power of polished techniques, but by my Spirit, saith the Lord of

11

Hosts" (Zec 4:6, free trans.). He has continually recognized that "no man can say that Jesus is the Lord, but by the Holy Ghost" (1 Co 12:3).

This new edition will be eagerly studied by all those who are seeking to improve the teaching ministry of the church.

HAROLD E. GARNER

Introduction

THE GREAT IMPETUS in the use of audiovisual media to assist in educational communication grew out of the circumstances surrounding the Second World War. Rather than using lecture alone, military instructors used visual demonstrations, films, and other media to prepare men for battle. Consequently, warfare techniques and strategy were learned far more quickly through this new approach to education.

However, before the war, educational researchers had already been hard at work studying how to communicate more effectively by using the eye-gate as well as the ear-gate. When the military was faced with the problem of educating a large number of men in a relatively short period of time, it began to build upon the research already completed. As a result, great strides were taken in developing and utilizing audiovisual tools.

Secular educators began to build upon the progress of the military, and many school systems started to make extensive use of audiovisuals. Motion-picture projectors, filmstrips, slide machines, overhead projectors, tape recorders and record players became standard equipment in many classrooms. Audiovisual centers were organized to assist teachers not only in using these media, but also in organizing their classroom curricula.

But educators have continued to advance in their concepts, and more and more breakthroughs have been made in the behavioral sciences as well as in technological fields. Video tape and tape cassettes have made possible unbelievable possibilities for creative teaching, all well within the reach of schools with limited budgets. "Gold-plated" retrieval systems utilizing the computer and costing a fortune can now be almost functionally duplicated with an inexpensive cassette program. And, of course, inexpensive video cassettes for educational purposes are now on the horizon.

One of the most recent and exciting concepts in education revolves around the learning center and individualized instruction. Programmed materials—both visual and auditory—tape cassettes and other media are used on a self-study basis, enabling students to individually master information that is normally taught in data-input courses. Teachers, rather than spend-

13

ing their time as "tape recorders wired for sound," can double their effectiveness by meeting students in small groups for interaction sessions based upon information that has already been learned on a self-study basis. Here the emphasis is on clarification, understanding and application, rather than just on transmission. In other words, more time can be spent by the teacher in helping students achieve attitudinal and behavioral goals, rather than just knowledge goals.

Here and there, Christian schools at all levels are beginning to catch the vision of what can be done with educational media. Christian publishers who have been in the business of preparing curriculum materials, particularly for use in Sunday schools, children's church, vacation Bible school, and youth meetings, have set the pace in developing media to communicate biblical truth. A number of churches and Christian schools have set up audiovisual centers to assist teachers in the use of these tools and materials.

This audiovisual handbook was first published in 1958 to assist Christians to make use of audiovisual media in their teaching. Since then it has been used in many churches as a resource guide, and in many Christian schools as a textbook in audiovisual courses. Though in many respects the original ideas are still ahead of many Christian education programs, the book has been thoroughly revised and updated to incorporate many of the latest concepts, techniques and tools which may be used to do a more effective job in Christian education.

GENE A. GETZ

1

Biblical Foundations

MANY YEARS AGO, John Amos Comenius discovered a principle of learning which is clearly evident in the Word of God—that people learn best through sensory experience.

Comenius was born at the Moravian village of Niwnic in the year 1592. While yet a child, he lost both parents, so his early years of education were neglected. But at the age of sixteen he had opportunity to study Latin, which created a great thirst for learning. With this thirst came the desire to help others to become "inflamed with the love of learning."[1]

Comenius was educated in German universities, and within his being developed a strong urge to improve educational endeavors. One of his primary emphases was "the importance of learning by sensory experience." He also became an ardent student of the Scriptures. At the age of twenty-four he was called to pastor a Moravian church at Fulneck.

Several years later great religious persecutions brought heartache and banishment to Comenius. He lost almost all he possessed as well as his wife and only child. But with a strong faith in God, he withstood the trials victoriously.

After fleeing his country, Comenius gave himself to studying and writing. His great burden for educational improvement was never thwarted. However, great persecution still lay ahead. He was never allowed to return to his native land, and many of his books and manuscripts were burned in Leszna, Poland. For a time he was homeless and faced illness and other misfortunes. But during the remaining years of his life he was given asylum in Amsterdam where he taught, studied and wrote. He died in the year 1671 at the age of eighty.

Although Comenius' life was filled with trouble, and though he did not live to see many of the educational improvements he so much desired, he never lost faith in God and the Scriptures. He was a man of aspiration; he worked hard until the close of his life.

Comenius' great emphasis upon sensory experience in learning is still considered basic, and many secular educational historians credit him as being the founder of the organized audiovisual movement. Believing that visual aids were foundational for good teaching, Comenius wrote,

> The sense of hearing should always be conjoined with that of sight, and the tongue should be trained in combination with the hand. The subjects that are taught should not merely be taught orally, and thus appeal to the ear alone, but should be pictorially illustrated, and thus develop the imagination by the help of the eye. Again, the pupils should learn to speak with their mouths and at the same time to express what they say with their hands, that no study be proceeded with before what has already been learned is thoroughly impressed on the eyes, the ears, the understanding, and the memory. With this object, it is desirable to represent pictorially, on the walls of the classroom, everything that is treated of in the class, by putting up either precepts and rules or pictures and diagrams illustrative of the subjects taught. If this be done, it is incredible how much it assists a teacher to impress his instructions on the pupil's mind.[2]

Many secular historians, although they credit Comenius as being the father of modern audiovisual movement, seldom make reference to the many biblical examples of visual instruction that were employed thousands of years ago. This is of no little interest since Comenius, according to Cubberley, "held the Holy Scriptures to contain the beginning and end of all learning."[3] It is easy for a Bible student to understand why Comenius believed in the value of sensory experience in learning, for a study of the Word of God reveals that God and His appointed teachers made extensive use of visual instruction. Comenius in his biblical studies evidently discovered that the Old Testament and New Testament are rich in examples of how visual aids have been used in Jewish and Christian education.

OLD TESTAMENT USAGE

When God created man, He placed within his being at least five basic senses. He enabled man to taste, to smell, to touch, to hear, and to see. In addition to creating man with these five senses, He gave him the capacity to enjoy them and to use them. One of the most profitable things man was enabled to do with his senses was to discover new things, to learn. After man sinned, God did not cease to make use of the senses He had created within man. He has used both the ear-gate and the eye-gate to bring man back to

Himself, to lead him into the truth of forgiveness of sin through Jesus Christ. It is but a simple matter to trace God's progressive revelation of Himself through the Old Testament into the full revelation of Jesus Christ as it is found in the New Testament. In this study it is easy to see how God used audiovisuals to relate this revelation to man.

For 120 years Noah labored to build an ark in response to a verbal commandment. After the flood, at the conclusion of his faithful ministry he was rewarded with a visual aid, a beautiful rainbow which God gave as a token of a covenant that He would never again destroy mankind with a flood (Gen 9:12-17).

When God told Abraham to leave his country and go to a strange land, he obeyed (12:1-4). With this commandment came a promise that he would be greatly blessed and would become the father of a great nation (12:2), and, in addition, all other nations would be blessed through him (12:3). Abraham took God at His word; but as the years went by, his faith grew weak for as yet he had no son (15:2). Could God's promise be fulfilled? He began to doubt. One evening God led Abraham out into the open country and spoke to him again. But this time He did more than speak to him. God said, "Look now toward heaven, and tell the stars, if thou be able to number them: and he said unto him, So shall thy seed be" (15:5). As a result of this visual demonstration combined with the reassuring words of the Lord, Abraham "believed in the Lord; and he counted it to him for righteousness" (15:6).

FROM EGYPT TO CANAAN

A most interesting study of God's use of visual aids is found in the account of the children of Israel as they journeyed from Egypt to Canaan. From the call of Moses to the crossing of Jordan, the Lord used visual demonstrations to accomplish His goals.

The call of Moses. One day as Moses was leading his father-in-law's flock of sheep to the backside of the desert, he saw a bush on fire. The sight was very strange indeed, for the bush was not consumed. Moses' curiosity was aroused. He said, "I will now turn aside, and *see* this great sight, why the bush is not burnt" (Ex 3:3). He did not realize that God was in the bush. Nor did he realize that God had used this bush to attract his attention so that He might speak to him. The burning bush, however, served its purpose well, for, "when the Lord saw that he [Moses] turned aside to *see,* God called unto him out of the midst of the bush, and said, Moses, Moses. And he said, Here am I" (3:4).

Moses was now ready to listen to the voice of God; he was attentive. His mind was no longer occupied with the sheep in the desert. God proceeded to speak to Moses and to tell him of the job He had for him, the great responsibility of leading the children of Israel out of Egypt. But even with such a great verbal and visual demonstration, Moses was quick to doubt his ability to accomplish such a great task. He objected by saying that the people would not listen to his voice. God quickly revealed to Moses that the job was not to be done in the strength of the flesh but in the strength of the Lord, the power that He would give. He gave Moses three visual aids to demonstrate this power. Not only was Moses to speak forth, saying that he had come with a message from God, but he was to use the rod which through the power of God would become a serpent and again be changed to a rod. He was to use his hand which would become leprous and again be made whole, and he was to use the water which would become blood when poured upon the ground. These visual aids would prove that Moses had a message from God (4:1-9).

Experiences in Egypt. Moses returned to Egypt, accompanied by his brother Aaron, who was chosen by God to be a spokesman for Moses. By using the visual aids which God had given, they soon convinced the children of Israel that the Lord had sent them to be their leaders (4:31). But in addition to convincing the Israelites of their mission, Moses and Aaron were faced with the task of persuading Pharaoh, king of Egypt, to let God's people go. Verbal symbols were not enough. Ten very forceful visual demonstrations were needed to convince Pharaoh that he should let the children of Israel leave the land (Ex 7—12).

The journey to Canaan. When the people of Israel finally left Egypt, God demonstrated His presence, power and protection in numerous visual manifestations. As they journeyed, He went before them in the pillar of cloud by day and in the pillar of fire by night (13:21). As they came to the Red Sea, the situation seemed impossible! The Egyptians were following close behind. At God's command, Moses stretched out his hand over the sea, the waters parted, and the children of Israel marched across on dry ground. Once on the other side, Moses again stretched forth his hand and the waters came together, drowning the Egyptians who had followed them into the midst of the sea (14:21-28).

As God's chosen people journeyed in the wilderness, God continued to meet their needs. At Marah the bitter water was made sweet when God led Moses to cast a certain tree into the water (15:23-25). When they were in need of food, God gave them meat in the evening and bread in the morning (16:10-15). Again when they needed water, God commanded Moses to strike the rock in Horeb, and water came forth (17:5-7).

Again and again God used visual aids to prove to the children of Israel as they journeyed to Canaan that He was their God and that He had not forsaken them. As they finally approached Jordan and as the priest entered the river with the ark of the covenant, the water stood up in a heap and all the people passed over on dry ground into the promised land (Jos 3).

Thus we see God using visual aids to teach the children of Israel. It is clear from Scripture that what God did and taught was not to be only an accumulation of vague and meaningless miracles and word symbols. He wanted them to be assured that He was their God and that He desired their love and obedience.

When Moses called together the children of Israel to give them his parting words just before they were to enter the land, he said, "Hear, O Israel, the statutes and judgments which I speak in your ears this day, that ye may *learn* them, and *keep*, and *do* them" (Deu 5:1). The commandments of God were to be meaningful—so meaningful that they would not forget them. They were also to be applied to their life experiences, for they were to "do them." Moses reminded them of the great audiovisual demonstration, including the trumpet, the thunders and lightnings, and the cloud which God used when He gave His statutes and judgments in the wilderness of Sinai (Ex 19:13-16; Deu 5:4-5). He called to their remembrance the "two tables of stone" which were given at that time with the commandments of God written upon them (Deu 5:22). Moses continued his exhortation by saying,

> And these words, which I commanded thee this day, shall be in thine heart: And thou shalt teach them diligently unto thy children, and shalt talk of them when thou sittest in thine house, and when thou walkest by the way, and when thou liest down, and when thou risest up. And thou shalt bind them for a sign upon thine hand, and they shall be as frontlets between thine eyes. And thou shalt write them upon the posts of thy house, and on thy gates (Deu 6:6-9).

Moses commanded that the words of God were to be taught "diligently" to the "children," not merely as verbal symbols without meaning, but as living truths in the course of everyday life. They were to be repeated again and again, and the lives of the parents were to demonstrate visually before the eyes of their children the meaning of these words. Learning was to result not only from *hearing*, but also from *seeing* and *doing;* there was to be application to life.

OBJECT LESSONS

A visual technique that is mentioned frequently in the Old Testament is the use of "symbolic acts" or "object lessons," a method used commonly by certain of God's chosen prophetic teachers.

Ahijah the Shilonite. After Solomon succeeded his father as king of Israel, he began to do evil in the Lord's sight by following after strange gods.

Because of this sin, God determined to rend most of the kingdom of Israel out of the hands of the seed of Solomon. While Solomon was still ruling over Israel, God made this known to Jeroboam, the son of Nebat, who was to be the first king over the Northern Kingdom. Jeroboam received this revelation one day while outside the city of Jerusalem.

> And it came to pass at that time when Jeroboam went out of Jerusalem, that the prophet Ahijah the Shilonite found him in the way; and he had clad himself with a new garment; and they two were alone in the field: And Ahijah caught the new garment that was on him, and rent it in twelve pieces: And he said to Jeroboam, Take thee ten pieces: for thus saith the Lord, the God of Israel, Behold, I will rend the kingdom out of the hand of Solomon, and will give ten tribes to thee (1 Ki 11:29-31).

Ahijah further explained to Jeroboam the significance of this object lesson. Naturally Jeroboam was greatly impressed. Evidently he returned to Jerusalem, told others what he had discovered, and the words eventually came to Solomon, who was so struck by the message that he immediately sought to kill Jeroboam, who fled to Egypt to save his life. There he stayed until King Solomon died. Hearing of Solomon's death, Jeroboam returned to Israel and soon was made king over ten of the tribes of Israel.

Ezekiel the dramatic prophet. Ezekiel, who used symbolic visual aids more than any other teacher mentioned in the Old Testament, has sometimes been called the "dramatic prophet." Many of the symbolic illustrations he gave Israel while in captivity were verbal; however, in several cases God commanded him to go before Israel to present literal object lessons.

In one instance (Eze 4:1-3), God told the prophet to take a "tile" or a piece of brick, to place it before him and paint on it the city of Jerusalem. He was to "lay siege against it, and cast a fort against it"; then he was to "set the camp also against it, and set battering rams against it." Thus Ezekiel was to picture for Israel an attack against Jerusalem. Furthermore, he was to take an iron pan and set it for a wall of iron between himself and the city; then he was to set his face against Jerusalem and lay siege against it. "This," said the Lord, "shall be a sign to the house of Israel."

In chapter 5 (vv. 1-3, 12) God confirmed what He had just taught regarding the siege of Jerusalem by commanding Ezekiel to use another object lesson. This time he was to use a razor to shave the hairs from his own head and his beard. Then he was to divide the hairs into three parts and weigh them in a balance. Next he was to burn one-third with fire, strike another third with a knife, and scatter the last third in the wind. This object lesson was full of meaning. Interpreted, it meant a third of the people would die from a pestilence and famine; another third would fall from the sword; and a third would be scattered to the winds.

These are but three of the object lessons or symbolic acts used by the prophets. They suffice to show how God used visual education in the Old Testament.

In New Testament history Jesus Christ Himself is the supreme example in the use of visual aids. Being the greatest Teacher who ever lived, He knew the value of using the eye-gate as well as the ear-gate. Here are a few outstanding teaching situations.

One day Jesus and His disciples were approaching the city of Capernaum in Galilee. The disciples, lagging some distance behind the Lord, became involved in a discussion which eventually developed into an argument. Arriving in the city, Jesus asked what had caused their dispute. Since they had been arguing about which one of them was to be greatest, they were ashamed to speak. Jesus, knowing all things, proceeded to teach them a lesson on the subject of humility. Since humility was an abstract term and a subject somewhat far removed from the present thoughts of the twelve, Jesus looked about for a concrete object to illustrate His lesson. Seeing a child, He called the little one to Himself and took him into His arms. With every eye upon the child, and every ear attentive, Jesus brought His lesson:

> Verily I say unto you, Except ye be converted, and become as little children, ye shall not enter into the kingdom of heaven. Whosoever therefore shall humble himself as this little child, the same is greatest in the kingdom of heaven. But whoso shall receive one such little child in my name receiveth me. But whoso shall offend one of these little ones which believe in me, it were better for him that a millstone were hanged about his neck, and that he were drowned in the depth of the sea (Mt 18:3-6).

Humility was no longer an abstract term to twelve sheepish disciples. What could have been more vivid and forceful than the use of such a verbal description and visual demonstration? The child became a perfect visual aid in the hands of the Lord.

This is but one of the many visual aids that Jesus used to lead men to Himself and to clarify truth. Again and again abstract truth was made clear and understandable by the use of a concrete object. To teach men to trust, He said, "Behold the fowls of the air" (Mt 6:26), and "Consider the lilies of the field" (6:28). In order to make clear the work of the Holy Spirit, He said, "The wind bloweth where it listeth" (Jn 3:8). To teach civic duty, He asked for a coin (Mt 22:15-22). Jesus believed in using visual materials.

It is evident that the theory and philosophy of visual education are rooted and grounded in the Word of God. It is not surprising that Comenius believed that, whenever possible, "the sense of hearing should always be conjoined with that of sight."[4] God ordained this principle in the Scriptures. When these two senses are used together effectively in a teaching-learning situation, the results will be most rewarding in terms of content learned and lives changed.

Yet there may be some well-meaning Christians who argue that although the principle of learning by sensory experience is scriptural, the Bible says nothing about using the modern audiovisual tools that are available today. "Who ever heard of the apostle Paul using a motion-picture projector or the Lord Jesus using a set of slides?" they ask. But it must be asked in return, "Who ever heard of the apostle Paul using an airplane in his missionary ventures, or of the Lord Jesus making use of the printing press?" The fact that these modern tools which are available today were not used in earlier times to preach the gospel in no way makes them unscriptural. Today, modern means of transportation are constantly used to carry on the work of the Lord. The same is true of up-to-date techniques of communication, such as the telephone and telegraph. Why not take advantage of developing technology to assist in teaching the Word of God? We have a biblical foundation for doing so.

Discussion Questions

1. Why is Comenius important in a discussion of the biblical foundation for using audiovisual media?

2. How does Satan use the senses of sight and of hearing to accomplish his goals today? Due to Satan's accomplishments, what serious objections may be raised by well-meaning people against the use of audiovisual aids in the church? Are these objections justified?

3. What additional illustrations can be given from the Scriptures to show the use of the audiovisual principle in communication? Consult the following passages: 1 Samuel 15:27-28; 1 Kings 19:19-21; 20:35-43; Psalm 19:1-6; Jeremiah 16:1-9; 19:1-15; 43:8-13; John 3:1-21; 4:1-41; 21:1-25.

2

Values

As I REFLECT back upon my academic experiences—from grade school to graduate school—I can isolate a number of teaching-learning situations in which I passed examinations and courses with flying colors. From all appearances I really *learned* from these experiences. My transcripts even record a number of A's.

But unfortunately some of these experiences were not as fruitful as they might appear. I can distinctly remember occasions when I fed back verbatim to the teacher ideas and concepts without any understanding whatsoever, and yet received a perfect mark on an exam.

OVERCOMING THE LANGUAGE BARRIER

My teachers faced one of the most difficult barriers to communication—the *language barrier*. God has chosen to reveal spiritual truths to mankind through the symbolism of written language in the Bible, the divine source for knowing about God, Jesus Christ, the Holy Spirit, salvation, Christian living and the other truths of the Christian faith. Jesus, when speaking to Thomas shortly before His departure to be with the Father, said, "Because thou hast seen me, thou hast believed: blessed are they that have not seen, and yet have believed" (Jn 20:29). Today Christ is not seen as the apostles saw Him, but He is revealed in the Word of God through word symbols which have been inspired by the Holy Spirit through the writers of Scripture. It is therefore vitally important that the meanings of these word symbols be made clear so that the learner truly grasps the intended message.

Edgar Dale, secular educator, has made a statement very apropos to this problem of effectively communicating the Word of God:

Helping students to attach the right names to objects and ideas is one of the teacher's essential jobs. When a concrete object is involved, there is little difficulty. But when we attach a name to an idea, a concept, an abstraction, the problem becomes complicated.[1]

Much of the content of Scripture deals with abstract truths, with terms such as Spirit, love, joy, peace, humility, grace and faith used to communicate them. However, unless the persons who are reading or listening to these terms possess some background of experience, the words will be meaningless.

MEMORIZING WORDS WITHOUT LEARNING MEANINGS

It is very possible to communicate word symbols without communicating the meanings that should be associated with the word symbols. Edgar Dale observes,

> As teachers, we quickly learn that students may react with verbal accuracy to questions about history or geography or mathematics, but that they sometimes don't know what they are talking about. Here is a boy who reads aloud about the Pilgrims. It sounds all right until a question shows that he does not know the difference between a Pilgrim and a turkey. He would be a fine one to send out to shoot a turkey.[2]

Herein lies a principle that is also applicable to Christian education. Careful evaluation will soon reveal that pupils may react with verbal accuracy to questions about the Bible, but often they do not know what they are talking about. The true test is what happens in a life situation.

Take the following incident: One Sunday morning Johnny, a four-year-old, was asked to repeat at home the memory verse he had learned that morning in Sunday school; he did so without hesitation: "Thou shalt love thy neighbor as thyself" (Mt 19:19b). He could repeat the verse with verbal accuracy.

During the following week, Johnny was outside playing with his new tricycle. Billy, who lived next door, came over to play with Johnny and asked to ride on his tricycle. When his request was refused, he tried to take the tricycle by force. Johnny, very displeased, hung onto his tricycle with all his might. Finally, in desperation, he hit Billy in the face with his fist. Billy, stunned and hurt, ran home crying as if his heart would break. Upon hearing the commotion, Johnny's mother came out of the house. Seeing what had happened, she regretfully said, "Johnny, I'm very displeased with you. What memory verse did you just learn in Sunday school?" Johnny unhesitatingly replied, "Thou shalt love thy neighbor as thyself." When questioned further it was evident that he saw no relationship between the Scripture verse and the experience he had just had with his neighbor, Billy.

This example illustrates one of the greatest problems faced by all Christian workers: the problem of communicating successfully. God in His Word has given the most important message in the world, but unless this message is effectively communicated to others it will not bring lasting results. It must, of course, be presented in the power of the Holy Spirit, but in addition, it must be presented to others so that it is understandable and meaningful. Only as it is taught clearly will meanings be grasped and spiritual concepts formed.

In order to see the full significance of this illustration it is necessary to analyze what happened in Johnny's Sunday school class the Sunday before this tricycle incident took place.

Johnny's teacher taught the verse to the class by having them repeat the verse after him. They repeated it again and again until every child could say the verse with verbal accuracy. No explanation was given as to the meaning of the verse, no effort was put forth to show how the verse was vitally related to the main aim of the lesson story that morning. No aids were used to help the boys and girls associate meanings with the word symbols. No discussion helped the children understand how this verse was related to their daily lives and experiences with other boys and girls. Consequently, the verse was memorized by rote but not understood.

What could have been done to make this Scripture verse meaningful? Many things are important at this point. Of course, the teacher should be well prepared for the entire lesson period. He should be able to tell the lesson story with enthusiasm, using words that are within the children's ability to understand. But a great aid in clarifying this verse and making it a part of each child's experience would be the use of visual aids, not only for the teaching of the verse, but throughout the Sunday school hour.

To illustrate, Johnny's teacher could have looked through the flat picture file or some magazines to discover several pictures illustrating "loving one's neighbor." He could have found pictures of children sharing toys, playing together, etc., which could have been placed on the bulletin board or on picture stands before the Sunday school session started. When the children came, the teacher could have led a presession discussion regarding the pictures and their meanings. He could have directed the discussion toward the lesson aim, that of "loving others." When the time came for learning the memory verse, "thou shalt love thy neighbor as thyself," the pictures could again be used. Perhaps the teacher could have asked questions such as, "Who are our neighbors? How are we to treat them? How can we show our love to them?" At this point the children could have come to the front one at a time and selected pictures that showed how they could love their neighbors. One would select a picture of "children playing together"; another would select a picture of "children sharing." Perhaps Johnny may even have found a picture of a boy "sharing his new tricycle" if the teacher had known of this new purchase and could have been prepared to use Johnny's personal experience as a vital teaching opportunity.

This, of course, is but one approach in teaching this memory verse in a meaningful manner. Various aids, such as the flannel board, a record, a filmstrip, the chalkboard, or concrete objects, could have been used. By actually visualizing what it means to "love one's neighbor as himself," these word symbols would have become understandable. Then, when Johnny was faced with the decision of showing this "love" to Billy, his "neighbor," the Holy Spirit could have used the verse Johnny had learned and applied it to his life experience.

LEARNING INCORRECT MEANINGS

Very closely associated with the language problem just mentioned, that of memorizing words without meaning, is the problem of misunderstanding which results in wrong conceptions. The ability to memorize Scripture, songs and prayers, or to listen attentively to a story or lesson, does not guarantee that the learner has grasped the correct meaning of the content. On the contrary, many illustrations can be given to prove that all ages are subject to misinterpretation. The following illustrations reveal actual misconceived ideas acquired by children:

In the song, "Dare to Be a Daniel," there is the phrase, "dare to have a purpose firm." Children have come home from Sunday school singing "dare to have a *purple spine*." Others have sung "*eat carrots for you*" rather than "He careth for you" or "**Gladly**, the *cross-eyed bear*" instead of "gladly the cross I'd bear." Children have actually placed their Bibles on the floor and have *stood* on them after singing, "The B-I-B-L-E, I *stand* alone on the Word of God." A boy came home from school one day and said, "Daddy, I want a *ruler* [referring to a twelve-inch ruler]; Jesus was a *Ruler*." And then, you can imagine the amazement of the parent who asked his child the meaning of the song, "Jesus wants me for a *sunbeam*," and received the reply, "Oh, that means a *Mixmaster* like Mother has on the kitchen shelf."

But what about adults? Many people are of the opinion that these mistakes are common only among children. A radio choir once received the request to repeat the song "Sweet *Peas*, the Gift of God's Love." In one issue of *The Sudan Witness*, a missionary periodical, a report was given illustrating similar requests from people who listened to a Christian radio station. In the article entitled, "Good Humor," the following "choice chuckles" were listed:

"In My Heart Rings a *Merry Bell*"
"Don't Forget to *Play*"
"When the *Sins* Go Marching On"
"Jesus Wants Me for a *Sunday*"
"*Jest* a Little with Jesus"
"*Flowers* of Blessings"
"*Father*, How Long"
"There's Not a Friend Like the *Lonely* Jesus"[3]

These mistakes *are* humorous, but beyond the humor lies a very serious problem because research reveals an endless list of these mistakes made by all ages. After speaking to a group of Sunday school teachers and officers on the subject of audiovisual aids, and illustrating the need for clarifying words and content, I was told this story by one of the group: She explained that when she was a very little girl, her father was a mailman. One day a lady on the mail route, who was quite dissatisfied with his service, told him she was going to have him "canned" if he didn't do a better job. The little girl overheard her father relating the experience to her mother, and for years she lived in the horrible fear that someday her father might be "cut up" and "put in a can."

Ridiculous? Yes, but very real to a little girl for several years of her life. This problem of misinterpretation and misunderstanding is a serious one which becomes even more serious when one realizes that the misunderstandings just illustrated are probably few in comparison with the vast number of biblical ideas that are not only misunderstood but missed altogether.

Audiovisuals aid greatly in overcoming the language barrier. Used properly, they will help to clarify the meanings of words and content. Meaningless memorization and misinterpretations of the Word of God must be kept at a minimum.

OVERCOMING THE TIME BARRIER

The Bible speaks of incidents that took place centuries ago when life and its many experiences were much different than they are in the twentieth century. Every teacher of the Word of God faces the problem of helping to bridge this gap in the minds of learners. Literally, one cannot go back to the time of Christ but, by using audiovisual aids, pupils are enabled to visualize what it was like two thousand years ago. Flannelgraph, flat pictures, filmstrips, slides, films, objects and models can make customs and experiences of biblical times understandable. Bible events can become alive and appealing, which is certainly not the case in many teaching situations today.

Overcoming the Space Barrier

Biblical events took place in a very small section of the world, far removed in distance and in cultural practices from this country. Those who are able to travel to the Holy Land in connection with biblical studies are few indeed and greatly privileged. But those who do not have this great opportunity are privileged today to be able to experience vicariously what it would be like to travel from Egypt to Canaan, or from Jerusalem to Capernaum in Galilee. This experience is made possible by the use of actual photographs, slides, filmstrips, and motion pictures. By using illustrated maps, one can visualize the journeys of the children of Israel, of Jesus and of the apostle Paul.

Audiovisuals *can* assist invaluably in solving the problems presented by the barriers to communication. Visual description can be combined with verbal description so that correct ideas are gained. Audiovisuals can aid in building concepts so that people—young and old—can have a better understanding of what is meant by the terms Holy Spirit, love, joy, peace, humility, grace, faith and salvation. They can provide a background of experience so that learners associate correct meanings with word symbols, avoiding the misconceived ideas illustrated earlier in this chapter. They can help bridge the gaps of time and space. In the words of F. D. McClusky, "Audiovisual materials 'speak' a universal language. They cut across language differences and barriers. Motion pictures in particular are valuable in communicating ideas that are understood universally."[4]

Making Learning Interesting

Understandable learning in itself is foundational in making learning interesting. Most people are not interested in learning that which has no meaning, nor do they enjoy the process. Furthermore, they will not be motivated to use what they have learned, for motivation results from learning that is understood and learning which touches the emotions and the will.

Audiovisual media help make learning interesting since they add *variety* to what is often a dull teaching-learning process. Experience has proved that learners respond well to teaching that makes extensive and effective use of the various types of audiovisual materials. Dullness and boredom can be kept at a minimum. Also, psychologically, it is easier to "see, listen, and participate" rather than just to listen to what Edgar Dale calls teachers "in love with the sound of their own voices, 'living textbooks wired for sound.' "[5]

Another reason why audiovisual aids make learning interesting is that they can provide *participation*. Students can help make and prepare visual aids by cutting out flannelboard figures, cutting out, mounting, and filing flat pictures, making posters, charts and graphs, preparing exhibits, and drawing maps. Older pupils can make flannelboards, easels and bulletin boards, devise special object lessons, take pictures, make slides, prepare filmstrips, mount pictorial material, and help prepare for observation trips.

Pupils can also participate in the actual use of visual aids. Children can tell the flannelboard story, manipulating the figures themselves. They can hold flat pictures or place them on the bulletin board, write on the chalkboard, decorate the bulletin board, hold a poster or chart, move a pointer on a graph, and point out various locations on a map. Older pupils can produce radio programs and operate tape recorders, phonographs and various types of projection equipment.

Audiovisuals provide for pupil participation in that they stimulate thought and discussion. Effective use of these aids provides for inner, active learning rather than allowing students to sit passively. All audiovisual aids should be used in such a way that pupils are made to think and, if possible, to participate in class discussion resulting in group interaction.

Another reason why audiovisual aids make learning interesting is that they induce real *incentive*. For example, a missionary film, filmstrip, or set of slides portraying the needs of the field can do far more than words alone in challenging people to go, give and pray. Mission graphs and flat pictures accompanying a missionary story can bring the challenge to children as well. Tape-recorded letters from the field, missionary maps, and many other audiovisual aids help to keep missionary interest high.

MAKING LEARNING RAPID AND PERMANENT

Experiments have demonstrated that it is possible to learn much more in a given period of time and to remember what has been learned for a much longer period of time when audiovisuals are used properly. For example, researchers have discovered that learning can be increased as much as 300 percent, with a reduction of more than 13 percent in teaching time.[6] Studies have also shown that the average learner remembers about 10 percent of what he listens to, and 20 percent of what he sees, but he remembers 65 percent if he both hears and sees.[7]

Edgar Dale has probably contributed more than any other educator in demonstrating the value of audiovisuals. On the basis of his own research as well as that of others, he has set forth these seven points to prove the contribution of audiovisual materials when they are used properly:

1. They supply a concrete basis for conceptual thinking and hence reduce meaningless word-responses of students.

2. They have a high degree of interest for students.

3. They make learning more permanent.

4. They offer a reality of experience which stimulates self-activity on the part of pupils.

5. They develop a continuity of thought.

6. They contribute to growth of meaning and hence to vocabulary development.

7. They provide experiences not easily obtained through other materials and contribute to the efficiency, depth, and variety of learning.[8]

In no other field should there be more concern in doing the best possible teaching job than in Christian education. Biblical materials need to be presented so as to be understood and applied to life. Learning God's truth should be a thrilling and challenging adventure; in these days of limited opportunities, as much as possible should be accomplished in the time allotted; wasted minutes should never exist.

Audiovisual aids, if used according to the principles suggested in this manual, will assist greatly in accomplishing these goals. The barriers of language, time and space can be minimized. Learning as well as teaching will become a meaningful, pleasant experience. There will be more learning in the time available, and the truths of the Scriptures will become a permanent part of life.

Discussion Questions

1. Think of several instances where the language barrier or the space barrier or the time barrier have been problems in your own experience. Could visual aids have been used to overcome these barriers? How?

2. Think of several high school or college experiences where the teaching-learning situation was very boring. Why was this true? Could audiovisual aids have added interest to these learning experiences? How?

3. In thinking back over learning experiences you had yesterday, last week, a year ago or perhaps several years ago, what facts and ideas do you remember most clearly? Why is this true? Do audiovisual aids play any part in this?

3

Root Problems

UNFORTUNATELY, knowing that the use of audiovisuals is rooted in Scripture and that science has demonstrated their value is not sufficient reason to motivate people to make use of these media. There is still a great lag between potential and practice. Though many excellent resources are available, many Christian teachers make little, if any, use of these aids in communicating the Word of God. The problem then, has deeper roots.

INSECURITY

One of the most subtle reasons for lack of creativity in teaching is insecurity—the fear to try new things. Over the years we develop teaching patterns with which we feel comfortable and secure. Aligned with these habits is the natural tendency to become rigid as we grow older. And closely related to and interwoven with these two factors is the spiritual problem of pride. The older we get, the more people expect of us, and our natural response is to continue to do things in a way in which we are sure we will not fail. And to admit there are new ways of doing things about which we know nothing is even a greater threat to our self-image. After all, we've been teaching for years!

Any teacher who falls into the trap just described is bound to continue doing things in the "same old way." If "talking" is his only method, he'll continue talking, for it is in talking that he feels successful and secure. You can demonstrate the biblical principle of verbalization plus visualization, pointing out the experimental evidence for more effective learning with audiovisuals, but his pride may keep him from breaking his old habit patterns.

At this point it is also easy for rationalization to set in. This type of individual may justify his behavior with selected biblical reasons. For example, one person used "Faith cometh by *hearing* and *hearing* by the Word of God" (Ro 10:17) and reasoned, "Is this not sufficient evidence that 'talking' and 'lecture' are the God-ordained means for communication?"

Of course, he had not so much as heard of Proverbs 20:12 which reads, "The hearing ear, and the seeing eye, the LORD hath made even both of them." And even if he had, he would not perceive the significance, for pride blinds us to our weakness.

Another outstanding excuse is that using various techniques and modern tools to communicate the Word of God tends to be a substitute for relying on the Holy Spirit. The most subtle aspect of this excuse is that it "sounds so spiritual." Who in his right mind would argue against this kind of reasoning?

The interesting facet to this excuse is that the person who rationalizes in this way proceeds full speed ahead to violate the creative nature of the Holy Spirit by being rigid and stereotyped in his approach to communication. There is abundant evidence in Scripture and history that the Holy Spirit is an infinitely creative Person who works in ways that are unpredictable and even beyond our ability to comprehend.

Who can accuse the Godhead of rigidity and stereotyped approaches to revealing eternal truth to mankind? The Bible itself is a constant tribute to God's creativity in communication. Though it represents just one way in which God has communicated with man, in itself it is a masterpiece in creative writing. Its contents include history, poetry, correspondence and a variety of other types of material. The genius and creativity of over forty authors were blended together in one harmonious whole which was inspired by the Holy Spirit. Various writing styles are evident from book to book, reflecting the personalities of individual authors, and a distinctive purpose is behind the writings of each book.

Insecurity, pride and fear of failure are some of the greatest barriers to creativity and to change in communicative techniques, and unfortunately Christians can sometimes be the most guilty of such behavior. This root problem must be solved if teachers and Christian leaders are to be creative, fresh, and up-to-date in their work and witness.

Regarding this problem, Dr. Francis Schaeffer makes a very significant comment in his book *The Church at the End of the 20th Century:*

> Refusal to consider change under the direction of the Holy Spirit is a spiritual problem, not an intellectual problem. There is a bad concept of old-fashionedness and there is a good concept. The good concept is that some things never change because they are eternal truths. These we must

hold to tenaciously and give up nothing of this kind of old-fashionedness. But there is a bad sense. I often ask young pastors and professors who are wrestling with these things a simple question: Can you really believe that the Holy Spirit is ever old-fashioned in the bad sense? The obvious answer is No. So if we as evangelicals become old-fashioned—not in the good sense, but the bad—we must understand the problem is not basically intellectual, but spiritual. It shows we have lost our way. We have lost contact with the leading of the Holy Spirit who is never old-fashioned in the bad sense.[1]

LACK OF INFORMATION

Not every person who "continues to teach in the same old way" is necessarily a victim of insecurity; rather, he may be uninformed. He doesn't know what the possibilities are. But reading about or being told about these possibilities is not enough, he needs to experience them. He may still be teaching the *way* he was taught, so he needs to experience learning that results from creative teaching.

This of course, has implications for leadership training. Jesus did not *tell* the disciples how to teach; He *showed* them. They learned through association, observation and practice.

Frequently leadership training is a process that involves verbalization about *how* to teach and not an experience *in* teaching. Naturally data input is important, for it *is* important to *know* how to teach. But creativity is learned through experimentation, trial and error, and actual practice—not just from reading books or from hearing a lecture.

It must be pointed out, however, that insecurity and pride are the greatest barriers to overcoming ignorance. A person can be so much in bondage to himself that he will not allow himself to be exposed to new ways of doing things. This in itself, he feels, is a reflection on his image. For after all, he reasons, if he admits that there are new things to learn, this reveals that he is not a competent teacher.

The opposite, of course, is true. To admit that there is more to learn—no matter what our age—is a sign of a mature and growing person. How sad it is when a teacher tries to cover up his incompetency by not allowing himself to be exposed to the solution to overcoming it. And the saddest part is that most people know what he is doing, while he alone feels he is covering up his problem. May God deliver us all from this kind of self-deception!

INADEQUATE PHILOSOPHY OF EDUCATION

Many Christian teachers—from the Sunday school to the seminary—do not have an adequate philosophy of education and do not understand the teaching-learning process. Consequently, methods and techniques in teaching are viewed from an improper perspective. Rather than seeing methods and media as a *means* to achieving biblical *ends*, they become ends in themselves. Rather than utilizing techniques naturally and spontaneously and in relationship to goals and the nature of the content, they use them mechanically and inappropriately. As a result, methods and media become gimmicks rather than *means* which are essentially related to the teaching-learning process. They use audiovisuals, for example, because someone says they should, rather than selecting teaching tools on the basis of what they want to accomplish in a given teaching situation.

People who function in this out-of-context manner become discouraged because they sense something is wrong. They quickly revert to their old ways, giving the excuse that these new approaches won't work. Rather than realizing that their failure is related to their inappropriate selection and use of various media, they put the blame on the media per se. This, of course, is a comfortable escape route but a sad commentary on the teacher.

Audiovisuals are not a quick and easy way to become an effective teacher, for they can only contribute to the teacher's effectiveness as they are used in context. They must be selected on the basis of the age level being taught and be utilized in relationship to teaching goals. Also, they must be used as a means to facilitate learning, not as an entertainment device or merely as an attention-getter. A teacher who has an adequate philosophy of education senses what tools are appropriate for a given situation, and when they will help rather than hinder communication.

LACK OF TIME

Perhaps one of the greatest hindrances to effective communication is the problem of time. It *does* take extra effort to make good use of the resources available today, and never before have people been so busy with a multitude of demands upon their time.

There is only one solution to this problem: establishing appropriate priorities. In other words, what is *most* important? As we put first things first, we will rise to the occasion and become effective communicators of the Word of God.

None of us needs to be reminded that we are living in a media-oriented society. All age levels are conditioned to expect the best in communication, and Christians cannot afford to be mediocre. We *must* rise to the occasion, and God forbid that we fail to do so because we will not take the time to put "first things first"—His things!

Discussion Questions

1. How can teachers who are threatened by technology and new ways of

teaching be helped to overcome this problem? Remember: You do not over-come your fear of water by being pushed off the dock!

2. How can teachers learn to teach by "experience" rather than by just being told *how* to teach?

3. What factors are involved in developing a biblical philosophy of educa-tion?

4

Objects, Models, Exhibits

ONE OF THE PROBLEMS in our technological age is that we tend to overlook some of the most effective media that are readily available—those things that are all around us and relatively inexpensive. These tools are sometimes more effective than anything else since they are familiar objects, and it is the familiar that assists in bridging the gap between the known and the unknown.

Looking through the Scriptures for the use of audiovisuals by biblical characters, it soon becomes obvious that they made use of whatever was available in the immediate external environment, such as a piece of tile, a tree, a bush, a piece of clothing, a child, a sower, water in a stream or well, or sheep grazing on a hillside.

OBJECTS

TYPES

Objects used as visual aids in Christian education may be defined as real things which can be observed by pupils and those things which help to clarify spiritual truths. A teacher may bring a beautiful bonquet of flowers or a growing plant to Sunday school to help children become aware of God's creative power. Various types of fruits and vegetables may be used. A bowl or a small aquarium with several fish and a bird in a cage will create further interest in God's creation and in the Word of God (see Figs. 1-2).

Missionaries who are home on furlough may use a variety of objects to acquaint people of all ages with customs of other lands. Curios of all types, such as baskets, weapons, cooking utensils, musical instruments, idols, religious ornaments and articles of clothing, create interest in the work being

Fig. 1. Discovering God through His creation (*Teach*)

Fig. 2. Observing the power of God (*Teach*)

done on the mission fields of the world. Churches with a real missionary vision will want to prepare special display cases to keep unique collections of missionary curios before the people. From this source, teachers will also be able to find special objects that will help to teach missions in the Sunday school and in other agencies of the church.

Then there are many interesting objects in God's animal, plant and mineral kingdoms which cannot be brought into class or department rooms. However, their spiritual significance can be seen by all ages as they go on planned observation trips.

Many common objects may be used symbolically. As illustrated in chapter 1, Ahijah the prophet used this type of object lesson to teach Jeroboam the truth regarding the division of the kingdom. Ezekiel used symbolic object lessons to warn of coming judgment. Common objects such as a coin, a match, a candle, or a piece of string may be used to great advantage. Many excellent "object lesson" books are available and should be used (see Appendix II). Most curriculum materials contain suggestions for preparing and using object lessons that will correlate with specific lessons.

One must be careful, however, not to use symbolic object lessons that are beyond the comprehension of the younger age groups. The fact that children may observe with interest does not mean they are grasping the spiritual meaning of the lesson.

In recent years symbolic object lessons known as "gospel magic" have grown to be quite popular. These object lessons, which range from the most complex professional tricks to simple acts which can be performed by any person, are being used in many areas of Christian education. A "bird cage" that disappears in midair may be used to illustrate the miracle of "sins forgiven"; a "bouquet" of beautiful flowers pulled from a hat may represent the beauty of the "Spirit-filled life"; a container of water that changes colors from black, to red, to clear due to certain chemical reactions may illustrate how the "blood of Jesus Christ . . . cleanseth us from all sin" (1 Jn 1:7).

Although these object lessons which involve mystery and trickery have seemingly brought good results in many cases, it is necessary to point out several problems. First, there is the possibility that small children may associate "supernatural power" with the performance of these magic tricks. Second, most children under the junior age are not capable of understanding the symbolic spiritual meanings which accompany the magic. Third, the mysterious element often detracts from the spiritual truth, even if it can be clearly grasped.

These problems do not imply that gospel magic should not be used. On the other hand, when used properly it can serve as an effective visual aid.

However, it is advisable not to use these object lessons with very young children.

Furthermore, when gospel magic is used with older age groups, the spiritual application should be made clear and meaningful, as even young people and adults have testified that they became so interested and fascinated with the mystery of the trick that they failed to grasp the spiritual meaning. At this point, gospel magic becomes purely entertainment, no longer a visual aid.

One might add that perhaps one of the greatest values of gospel magic *is* entertainment, and it is frequently used with great success as an evangelistic tool to build bridges with a non-Christian audience.

Fig. 3. A "touch and see" object (*Teach*)

Fig. 4. A "look and see" object (*Teach*)

PRINCIPLES FOR USE

1. Make sure that all can see.

2. Let pupils touch objects; this creates greater interest and helps to make objects more meaningful (see Fig. 3).

3. Use objects that will fit naturally into the lesson or unit of study; select them on the basis of appropriateness and need.

4. Don't use too many objects within one lesson; this may confuse rather than aid learning.

5. Make sure the object lessons are clearly understood; a good criterion is to let pupils explain the spiritual truths that they have learned.

1. Use observation trips whenever possible (see chap. 5).

2. Bring to the class or department room any object that will help clarify spiritual truths (see Fig. 4).

3. Let pupils bring their own objects to church or Sunday school. Encourage them to create their own object lessons that will fit into the lesson being studied.

MODELS

Whereas objects may be defined as *real things*, models differ in that they *represent* real things. Children, young people, and even adults enjoy making and playing with models. All ages spend hours constructing model planes, ships, houses, towers, and many other things from building blocks, clay, and other materials. It is still a question as to who enjoys the electric train more—Junior or Dad.

There is great value in the very process of making things! Since children learn by doing, models serve as excellent visual aids, whether prepared by the teacher or the pupils. Public schools are making extensive use of models in teaching and there is also marvelous opportunity in using them in the educational work of the church.

Materials and instructions for making models may be purchased from religious supply stores, but very excellent models may be originated and constructed by leaders and pupils. Most children and young people will never have the opportunity to actually see the Holy Land, but they can have a vicarious experience of seeing this land by constructing a large relief map of Palestine. They may never visit a mission field except as they see it portrayed on the screen by means of motion pictures, but they can enjoy a profitable learning experience by making a model of a mission compound or by constructing a miniature African village. Boys especially will enjoy making a model of a missionary radio station. Then there is the tabernacle in the wilderness which can be constructed and used again and again to teach New Testament as well as Old Testament truths. With guidance,

Fig. 5. Model of town of Bethlehem from papier-mâché

Fig. 6. A scale model of the tabernacle (Regier)

Fig. 7. A sand table or box is an inexpensive but very effective way of illustrating a biblical scene (Regier)

young people can study the instructions for making the tabernacle as they are given in the Scriptures and then make a scale model (see Figs. 5-6).

SAND TABLES

Sand tables are often thought of as visual aids that are appropriate only for use with children, but during the war the army made extensive and profitable use of them to illustrate strategy and to show important geographical locations.

The sand table does, of course, have a particular use with children. (See Fig. 7). With guidance they can construct scenes that took place on a mountainside in Galilee, by the seashore, or in their own community. Sand dampened with water is very workable. Bodies of water or rivers can be represented by using mirrors or strips of blue construction paper, while figures can be made from pipe cleaners or represented by small sticks or toothpicks. Calvary's hill with the three crosses against the sky outside Jerusalem can be easily constructed to help children visualize and experience the realism of those hours. Thus the sand table provides innumerable opportunities to make biblical and related scenes live for children.

Sand tables also have a unique ministry among young people and adults. A relief map of Palestine prepared on a sand table with model figures and small blocks of wood or buttons to represent cities and other locations will help older groups to visualize the Holy Land. The gospel accounts will come alive with this type of visual aid. Likewise, the Old Testament stories and the journeys of Paul will take on new meaning. A reproduction of "Operation Auca" on a sand table to help people visualize the efforts and martyrdom of the five young missionaries of Ecuador will provide an informative and impressive experience for young and old alike.

DIORAMAS

Dioramas provide excellent learning experiences when pupils make and view them. They may be defined as models which give a realistic three-dimensional effect (see Appendix IV for film suggestions).

For example, a shoe box may be prepared to look like the inside of a church. Small squares can be cut out of the inside walls and the top of the box and then covered with colored cellophane to represent stained-glass windows. The rest of the interior can be painted a light color to help give the desired effect. Small model pews and other fixtures made from scraps of soft wood or cardboard can be included to add to the realism of the diorama. A small hole cut in the back will allow pupils to view the scene inside. If more light is desired, small fixtures can be prepared with flashlight bulbs and a dry-cell battery.

Fig. 8. A teacher guides children in making creative visuals (*Teach*)

Fig. 9. Children observe a bulletin board display of creative work—done by their classmates (*Teach*)

Fig. 10. A teacher uses a simple hand puppet made from fabrics (*Teach*)

Much larger dioramas can be made of either indoor or outdoor scenes. A large painted background of a mountain, a forest, or other scenic view used with a small model mission station in the foreground will create missionary interest among those who construct it as well as those who view it.

These suggestions are just samples of innumerable dioramas which can be prepared for all ages. A visit to a modern museum will supply Christian workers with many excellent ideas for preparing and constructing dioramas for use in all areas of Christian education.

CREATIVE ACTIVITIES

In order to provide incentive for further study in the field of creative activities, the following list has been included to give suggestions as to common materials that may be used in preparing all types of models, including puppets, sand-table scenes, dioramas, and innumerable types of other creative activities (see Figs. 8-10).

bottles	marbles
bottle caps	matchboxes
blocks	mirrors
bricks	nails
cotton	paints
clay	paper cups
corrugated paper	paper plates
cardboard	paper sacks
clothespins	papier-mâché
colored construction paper	rocks and stones
crepe paper	sawdust
dirt, sand, mud	scraps of lumber
fabrics	shells
feathers	thread spools
fruit jars	tin cans
fruit jar lids	typewriter spools
fur	toothpicks
leather	wooden boxes and crates
magnets	

SUGGESTIONS FOR USE

1. Be aware of opportunities for pupils to construct models individually and as a group. Give careful guidance as pupils construct elaborate models without cramping their creative abilities.

2. Have older groups construct models to be used with children.

3. Add motion to models. Older young people who are studying me-

chanical subjects in high school will be able to prepare models that have moving parts.

4. Let pupils touch and operate models whenever possible.

Exhibits

A well-prepared exhibit will make a worthy contribution in helping to accomplish the work of the church. Used in Christian education, it may be defined as a group of objects, models, and other audiovisual aids arranged in orderly fashion so as to emphasize a single theme and to present a clear spiritual message to observers.

using exhibits

There are many opportunities for using exhibits. Parent-teacher meetings, vacation Bible school demonstration programs, and special exhibit nights all provide occasions for children and young people to display before parents and friends their handwork projects and other interesting objects and accomplishments (see Fig. 11). A special exhibit may be planned by a group of Sunday school children to summarize their unit of study on the life of Christ. Such an exhibit might include pictures, a relief map, a Bible, a tape recording, a poster, and handwork prepared by individual pupils. A whole

Fig. 11. An exhibit prepared by a group of children to demonstrate their study of creation (*Teach*)

department room can be arranged attractively for parents to see some of the accomplishments that have been made in two weeks of vacation Bible school. A group of young people can prepare a Bible exhibit showing the various translations of the Bible and other interesting facts by means of captions, pictures, charts, and projected aids.

The opportunities for the preparation of these visual aids are many. Planned and prepared well, they can be used effectively to win the friendship of uninterested parents and eventually to win them to Christ. Children and young people will also get great satisfaction from preparing exhibits, and their parents will be gratified to see their accomplishments.

Youth and adults can prepare exhibits to be used effectively at special youth rallies, Sunday school conventions, evangelistic meetings, and missionary conferences. Books, pamphlets, quarterlies, posters, films, filmstrips, slides, recordings, photographs, maps, graphs, charts, objects, curios, and other types of curriculum materials may be placed on display. Exhibits should also be used at local Sunday school teachers' and officers' meetings. A suggested plan is to prepare quarterly exhibits to display suggested helps and ideas that can be used by the teachers in the coming three months (see Figs. 12-15).

In many areas, especially in small towns and rural areas, young people and adults may obtain permission to prepare exhibits for use at county and local fairs. A large banner spread across the front of an exhibit booth will attract the attention of people passing by. Tracts and other free literature may be made available, and Bibles, Scripture portions, and good Christian books may be sold. Records of hymns and gospel songs can be played over a loud speaker, and special films and filmstrips can be shown periodically. Short attractive messages could be played on the tape recorder, and small filmstrip viewers may be used to attract attention. Good filmstrips with a silent message may be placed in these viewers and made available for interested people.

PRINCIPLES FOR PREPARATION

1. Prepare exhibits with a central theme.
2. Keep exhibits fairly simple; too many ideas confuse rather than clarify.
3. Consider who will be viewing them.
4. Provide opportunity for people to participate as they observe exhibits. This may be in the form of pushing a button, viewing a filmstrip, turning a handle, taking free literature, buying a book, etc.
5. Organize exhibits in an interesting fashion. If a great number of people will be seeing exhibits, arrange them so that traffic can be moved along easily without confusion.

Fig. 12. A missions exhibit (*Teach*)

Fig. 13. An exhibit on the Christian home (Regier and Miller)

Fig. 14. A leadership
training exhibit
(Regier and Miller)

Fig. 15. A children's book display (Regier and Miller)

6. Make sure that all can see adequately.

7. Use color to add attractiveness to exhibits.

8. Make sure that lettering is done neatly and attractively. Special lettering materials may be obtained for this purpose. Also, prepare labels that will describe individual work clearly.

9. Add movement whenever possible. This may be accomplished by using an electric fan, small electric motors, or regular display turntables.

Discussion Questions

1. In teaching the following lessons to a group of juniors (ages 9-11), what simple objects could be used to make the lessons more interesting and clearer to the pupils?

   a. the creation (Gen 1)

   b. David and Goliath (1 Sa 17:31-51)

   c. feeding the five thousand (Jn 6:1-14)

   d. the stoning of Stephen (Ac 7:54-60)

   e. the crucifixion (Lk 23:27-49)

2. In teaching the same lessons to a group of young people or adults, could the same objects be used? Why or why not? What additional objects could be used?

Special Projects

1. Make several of the following models:

   a. an African village

   b. a church

   c. an Oriental house

2. Make a diorama that could be used to teach a Bible or missionary story.

3. In preparing an audiovisual exhibit for a group of Sunday school teachers, what could be included and how could it be arranged? Prepare a diagram (to do this it may be necessary to scan the contents of this book).

5

Observation Trips

VERY FEW of the teaching-learning situations mentioned in the Bible took place in what we think of as a classroom today. Jesus, the master Teacher, taught His most unique lessons on a mountainside, by the seashore, or on a trip from one city to another where He could illustrate His teaching by referring to the many living and inanimate objects which He Himself had created (Jn 1:3).

Unequaled opportunities for relating Christian teaching to life experience are provided by study trips. Some trips will focus the spiritual needs of the world, while others will reveal God's greatness as seen from His marvelous and beautiful creation. Still others will show His love toward mankind as His natural provisions for the existence of life are observed. All field trips will provide opportunities for pupils to practice Christian graces as they associate with classmates and other people they meet.

Observation trips may be defined as excursions or journeys to any destination outside of the regular meeting place or classroom. They are one of the most valuable visual techniques of the church, yet many Christian teachers and workers never take advantage of this opportunity (see Appendix IV for film suggestions).

OBSERVATION TRIPS FOR CHILDREN

Boys and girls may make planned visits to other parts of their own church building. For example, as a group they may visit the morning worship service of the church to learn what it really means to worship God, or meet with the pastor during the week as he explains the various parts of the sanctuary. Together they may attend the weeknight prayer meeting, or a

51

Fig. 16. Looking at
what is available

Fig. 17. Listening to
a good story

A field trip to the
church library (*Teach*)

Fig. 18. Browsing
on their own

Fig. 19. Taking a
book home

communion or baptismal service. They may go to another department in the Sunday school to see how other boys and girls older or younger than themselves worship God, or to worship with them. They may also be conducted on such an excursion to prepare them for promotion from one department to another. A very interesting trip could be planned to the church office to discover how they can help the secretary. A planned visit to the pastor's home would be a very impressive and profitable experience for not only the children, but also for the teacher and minister (see Figs. 16-19).

Children may also visit points outside the church building such as nearby parks or the zoo to see the flowers, grass, trees, clouds, sky and many kinds of animals which God has made. Through such experiences, they may truly learn and more vividly realize what the psalmist means when he says, "The works of the LORD are great" (Ps 111:2).

OBSERVATION TRIPS FOR YOUNG PEOPLE AND ADULTS

A trip to a farm can make biblical settings in both the Old and New Testaments become more vivid and understandable. Parks and resorts provide excellent opportunities for nature studies. Museums, aquariums, planetariums and other similar places provide hundreds of visual lessons related to biblical and extrabiblical subjects, such as the creation story as opposed to the theory of evolution, the Bible and science, ancient customs, and man's increased knowledge and discoveries. In a study of missions and evangelism, a trip to a printing plant to show what is being done in the area of printing Bibles would prove profitable. This would also correlate well with a study of the Reformation and would show how the printing press aided its progress. In a study of the life of Christ or the apostle Paul, a visit to a Jewish synagogue would be worthwhile. However, be sure permission is granted by parents and pastor, and that those in charge at the destination have been informed and permission obtained. Make your purpose clear to all; you are making the visit to observe and not to criticize or to argue.

Young people need to know what true worship is, what the Bible says about true worship, how others worship, and how to worship in "spirit and truth." In connection with such a study, a trip may be taken to another church or several churches to see how various worship services differ and to observe the worship atmosphere. Observations of the physical structure of the church and arrangement of the sanctuary will also help in this study. The following illustrates how this idea was used in a young people's group:

On a weekend youth retreat, a young people's group decided to conduct a series of studies on the subject of "worship." Time was to be given to the study of the various elements included in a true worship service, such as Scripture reading, prayer, music and stewardship. At the conclusion of three months of study, smaller groups from within the larger group, after consulting their own pastor, went to visit other church services on several Sunday mornings. In the evening meetings of the young people's group, a report on what they had observed was given by the groups who had visited. After the reports, an open discussion was held or a planned message given covering the good points of the worship services and those points that needed correction. There was further discussion as to how these findings could be applied to the lives of the young people. These observation trips proved very helpful in illustrating true scriptural worship.

When a teacher is instructing young people regarding God's perfect will for their lives, there are many places which groups may visit. Some of these include Bible schools, Christian and secular colleges, Bible conferences, and resorts where weekend retreats can be held for a special spiritual challenge. Other places, such as rescue missions, offices of mission boards, hospitals, jails, orphanages, and rest homes also provide opportunities to motivate for Christian service.

Then there is the observation trip which aids greatly in promoting new ideas and suggestions for a better or new church building, a better organized Sunday school, or an up-to-date Christian education program. Leaders in the church assigned to a building committee are often challenged greatly by a visit to a new building already in operation, or teachers in the Sunday school are greatly impressed by a visit to a Sunday school that is "really going places." People are often convinced and led to action when they "see" that ideas work in actual situations.

Planning Observation Trips

It should be noted that the age of the group and the destination determine the type of planning needed for observation trips. A "short trip" within the church or just outside the building requires fewer details in planning than do trips to distant places. Then, too, a trip for children may be more teacher-centered in planning and guidance, whereas a trip for young people and adults may require just as much teacher preparation but more actual participation in planning by the pupils themselves. In general, however, the suggestions that follow are applicable to most age groups and all types of trips.

TEACHER PREPARATION

1. Choose a destination for an observation trip that will correlate with a particular lesson or with a unit of study.

2. Talk over the plan with the pastor and the director of Christian education. Get their ideas and reactions.

3. Contact the person in charge at the destination of the trip and secure permission to come.

4. Inform parents of all plans and secure their written permission when traveling to any point removed from the building.

5. Think through all problems such as distance, transportation, time, expense, age range of group, number in group, leaders needed, etc.

GROUP PREPARATION

1. Have pupils participate in the preparation for the observation trip.

2. Choose aims for the trip as a result of group discussion.

3. Decide on questions that need to be answered while on the trip.

4. Place helpful literature in the hands of the pupils which will prepare them for what they will observe.

5. Emphasize the importance of Christian courtesy and conduct while on the trip.

6. Appoint committees to help plan trips. The following are suggested: transportation, food, clothing, conduct and expense committees.

TAKING THE TRIP

1. Make sure parental consent has been obtained.

2. Maintain order.

3. Draw attention to particular points that should not be missed.

4. Stick to the planned time schedule.

FOLLOW-UP

A trip should not just be taken and then forgotten. Actual follow-up in the classroom after the trip is essential to gain the full value of time and effort involved and to make the lessons learned a part of the pupils' individual lives.

Class discussion. Discuss the answers to the questions given prior to the trip. In addition, evaluate the trip as a class by answering such questions as:

1. Was the trip a success? Why?

2. Were our aims reached? What did we actually learn?

3. Did we have enough time?

4. What changes need to be made for the next trip?

5. Was a good Christian testimony maintained?

SPECIAL PROJECTS

1. After visiting a morning worship service, a junior group of boys and girls may be led to plan and conduct their own service. Perhaps a plan for a junior church can be drawn up and put into action.

2. Older young people, after visiting other churches, may write their own worship services and present them. Afterward they can evaluate the effectiveness of their programs on scriptural grounds.

3. A group which has visited another department within the church may utilize special ideas for fixing up their own department or classroom.

4. After a visit to the great out-of-doors, children can plant seeds and watch them grow. Some can be watered; others not. Some can be placed in the sunshine and others left in the shadowy parts of the room. They can observe the importance of the sunshine which God has given and the rain that falls. They can also watch the growth from week to week. Many excellent spiritual applications can be made.

5. Young people and adults, after visiting other churches or a synagogue, may be led into further Bible study to discover what the Scriptures have to say about what they have observed.

6. Special skits, scrapbooks, charts, diagrams, posters, picture displays, etc., can be prepared by junior-age groups and older youth after various types of observation trips have been taken.

7. A day at a Bible conference can be influential in promoting a special youth missionary conference or evangelistic meeting in the church.

8. A visit to a rescue mission or a jail may challenge young people to organize a gospel team.

9. A trip to the office of a mission board or a missionary conference may challenge a group of young people or adults to raise their missionary budget and to promote a greater program of missions in the church.

10. A visit to an orphanage or a needy area can challenge young people and adults to start a clothing or food drive to help meet discovered needs.

Discussion Questions

1. What are the values of observation trips as compared with other types of audiovisual aids?

2. Discuss several trips that could be taken in your own church community. What are the values? Would they justify the time and effort involved?

Special Projects

1. Plan an observation trip. Select a specific age group, a specific lesson or unit of study, and a destination. Using the following outline, write out the plan:

    a. What is the aim or purpose of the trip?
    b. What is the age group?
    c. What is the lesson or unit of study?
    d. What is the destination?

    e. How would you prepare yourself as the teacher or leader?

    f. How would you prepare your pupils?

    g. How would you follow up the observation trip?

2. As a class, take an observation trip to discover additional information regarding the use of audiovisual aids. Plan the trip carefully as a group and put into practice the principles included in this chapter. Following is a list of places to go on trips:

    a. a radio station

    b. a store where audiovisual equipment and materials are sold

    c. a company that makes some type of audiovisual equipment or materials (such as recording tape)

    d. a public school where there is a well-organized audiovisual program and media center

    e. a church that has an audiovisual library and a "going" program

    f. a museum to see the many audiovisual aids that are used in presenting information

6

Graphics

I REMEMBER AS A BOY attending Sunday school and hearing about various Bible towns and places, both in the Old and New Testaments. I could readily answer many questions about various geographical facts, but I later learned I had no visual concept of the Bible lands. Consequently, my biblical perspective lacked continuity and I saw few interrelationships between events. For example, I saw no relationship between the land of David's day and that of Jesus Christ. As far as I knew, these two geographical settings may have been at opposite sides of the world.

As far as I can remember, I hardly ever saw a map during my Sunday school days, and very seldom ever saw one used when I attended Bible school and college, outside of a special course in Bible geography. This is very strange indeed when most of the biblical record is woven around geographical settings.

The same is true regarding charts and graphs. Most of my teachers simply did not use them. I suppose they were not aware of the great potential these media have in clarifying concepts and in making the Word of God clear and practical.

MAPS

Many excellent Bible and missionary maps may be purchased from religious supply stores. Some are designed for different age groups, taking into consideration pupils' abilities and progress in the public schools. Maps of the exodus, Palestine during the time of the judges, Palestine during the time of Christ, the Roman Empire, Paul's journeys, etc., are available. They

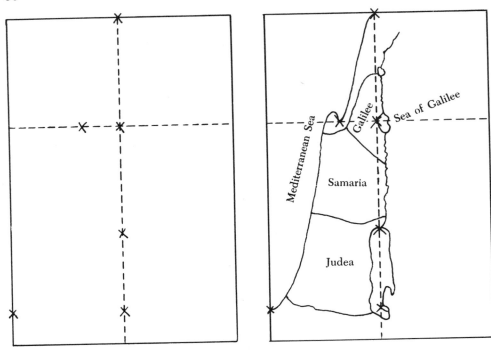

Fig. 20. Drawing a map of Israel

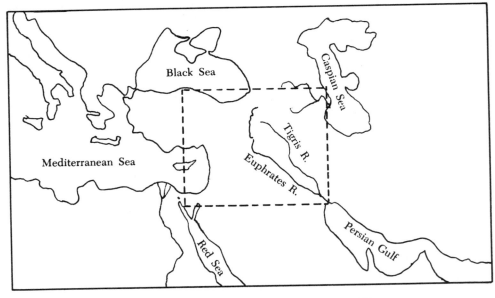

Fig. 21. Drawing the Old Testament world

may be purchased in different sizes and colors; others can be colored by the teachers or pupils. There are maps for flannelboards as well as three-dimensional maps. World missionary maps show the places where various religious groups are most active.

Some producers of curriculum materials also suggest and supply maps for certain studies. Large world maps and globes may also be purchased from secular stores that specialize in handling graphic materials. Excellent free materials may be obtained from sources such as airline and railroad companies.

Inexpensive maps may be prepared by teachers and pupils. The experience gained in planning and preparing these maps will provide much more opportunity to learn than the experience of just studying maps prepared commercially.

DRAWING FREEHAND MAPS

Teachers may use several techniques to draw fairly accurate freehand maps. The following suggestions are merely for extemporaneous drawings in the classroom; with practice, every teacher can use these techniques adequately.

Israel in the time of Christ. Follow these instructions:
1. Draw a cross lightly onto the chalkboard or drawing paper.
2. Mark six locations as illustrated in Figure 20.
3. Fill in the map, using the marked points as guides.

  a. Draw the boundary of the Mediterranean Sea.

  b. Draw the Sea of Galilee, making sure that the middle of the left side of the sea touches the marked point.

  c. Draw the Dead Sea, using the marked point as the upper tip of the sea.

  d. Add the remaining details of the map. The border lines of Galilee, Samaria and Judea are easy to locate after the other details have been drawn.

4. Use this map often in teaching the life of Christ. Additional points of interest, such as cities and other countries, may be added by consulting a Bible atlas or other maps.

The Old Testament world. Draw a rectangle as illustrated in Figure 21. The rectangle should be located approximately in the center of the map. The four points of the rectangle will serve as guides in drawing in the major details of the map.

The Sinai Peninsula. Draw a parallelogram as illustrated in Figure 22. Make sure it is to the right and slightly above the center of the map. The details of the map can then be easily and quickly sketched.

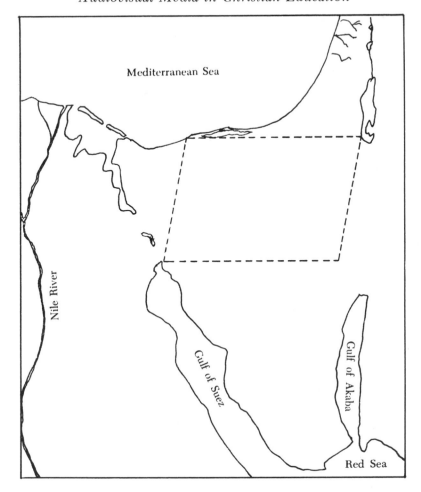

Fig. 22. Drawing the Sinai Peninsula

PREPARING OUTLINE MAPS

Maps can be prepared by using an opaque projector, a pantograph, and proportional squares as described in chapter 8, covering nonprojected still pictures. The same principles for drawing sketches apply in enlarging maps and in tracing them on drawing paper, the chalkboard, acetate for overhead projection (see chap. 9), or on other backing such as inexpensive light-colored window shades.

Following is a series of outline maps which can be traced, enlarged, or reproduced in other formats and used to teach the Bible more effectively (see Figs. 23-40).

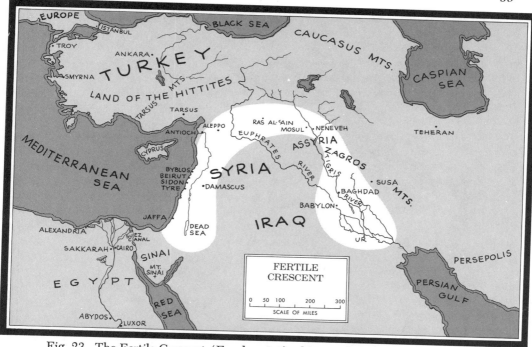

Fig. 23. The Fertile Crescent (For descriptive historical and geographical detail and assistance in using these maps see Charles F. Pfeiffer and Howard F. Vos, eds., *The Wycliffe Historical Geography of Bible Lands* (Chicago: Moody, 1967), pp. 1-2, 28-29, 34, 48, 56, 90, 97, 127, 136, 147, 187, 216, 239, 312, 346, 356, 388).

Fig. 24. Babylonian Empire

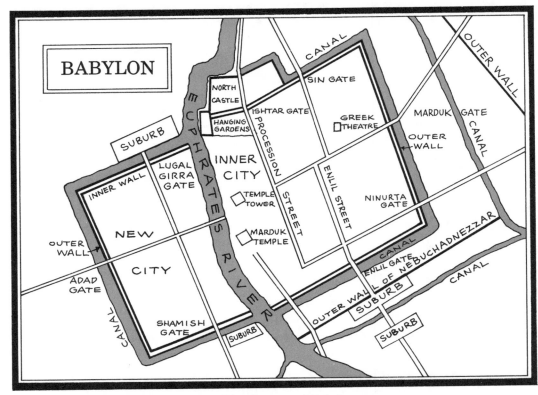

Fig. 25. The city of Babylon

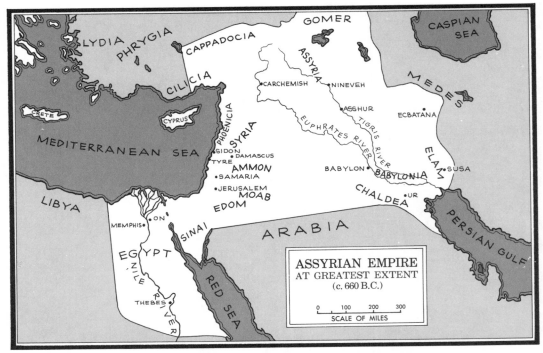

Fig. 26. The Assyrian Empire at greatest extent

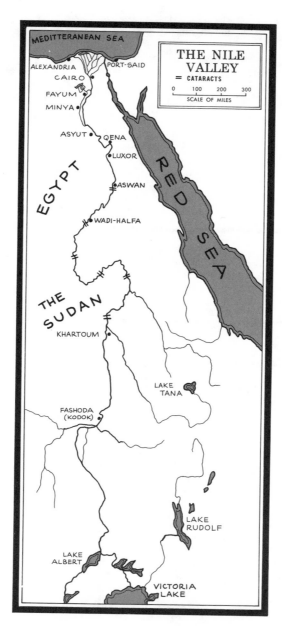

Fig. 27. The Nile Valley

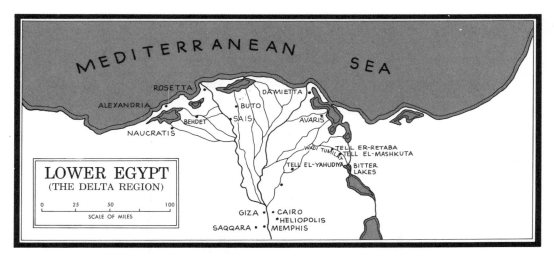

Fig. 28. Lower Egypt—the Delta region

Fig. 29. Route of the exodus

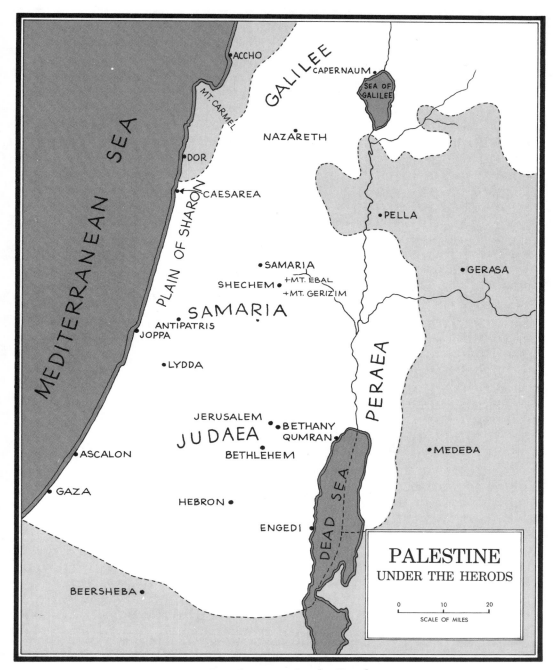

Fig. 30. Palestine under the Herods

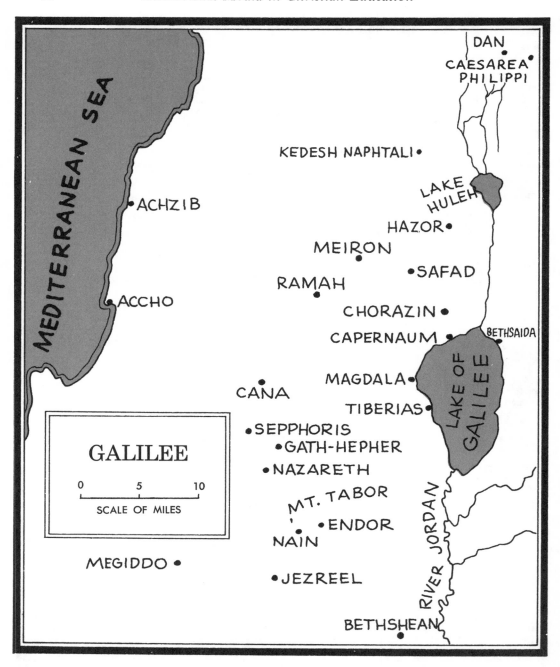

Fig. 31. Galilee

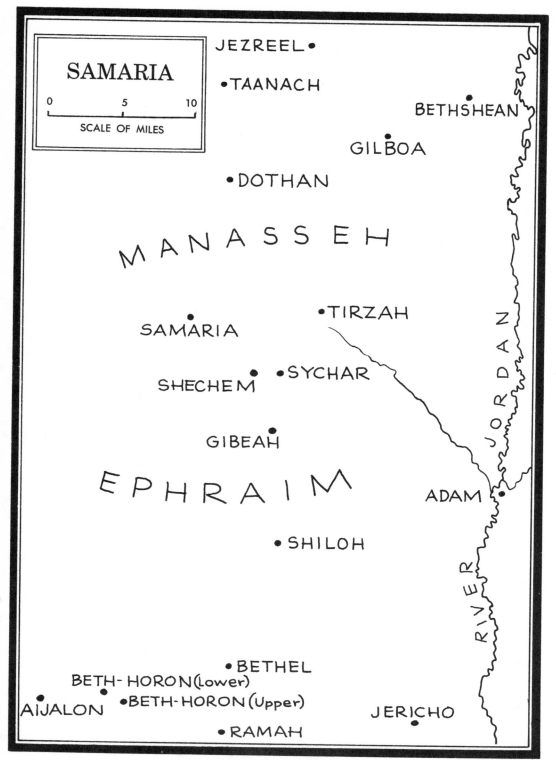

Fig. 32. Samaria

Fig. 33. Judea

Fig. 34. Phoenicia

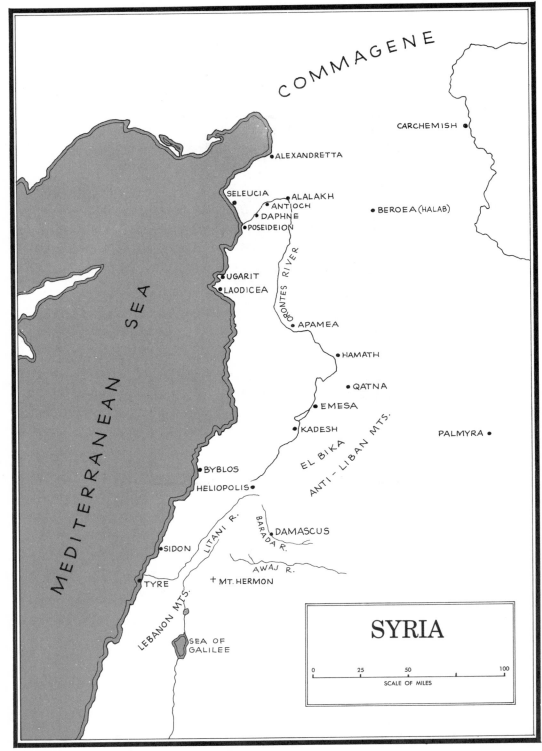

Fig. 35. Syria

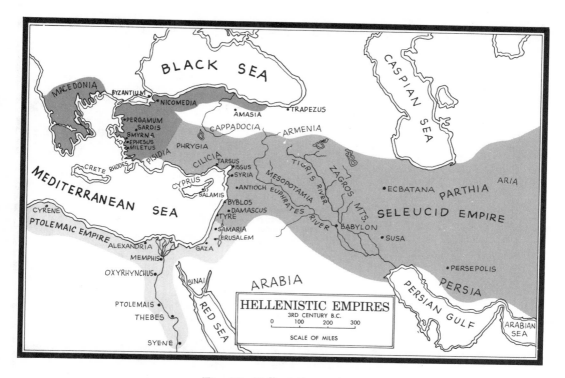

Fig. 36. Hellenistic empires

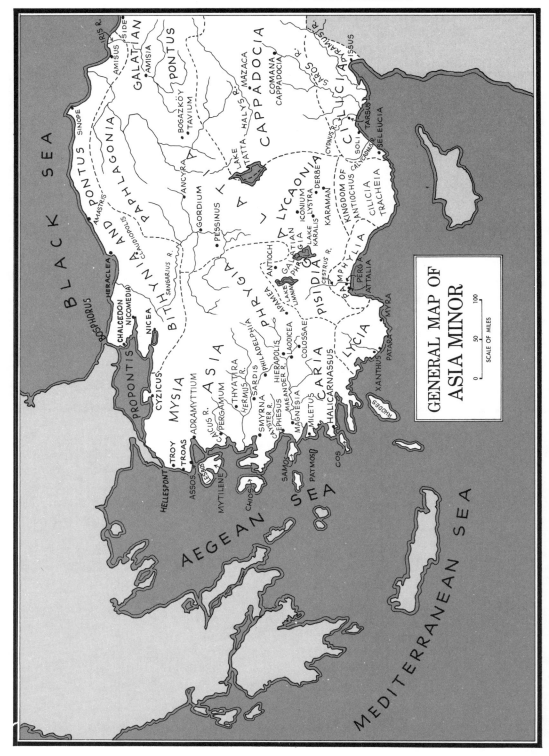

Fig. 37. General map of Asia Minor

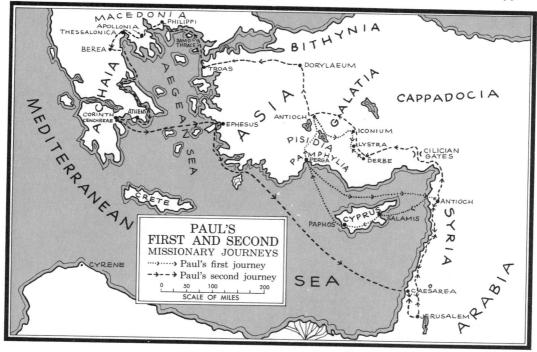

Fig. 38. Paul's first and second missionary journeys

Fig. 39. Paul's third journey and trip to Rome

Fig. 40. Seven churches of Asia

FLANNEL MAPS

Bible and world maps can be drawn or traced on pieces of flannel and used on flannelboards. Flannel maps have the advantage of allowing teachers and pupils to place flannel-backed figures and objects in different places. For example, the major countries and cities of Palestine in the time of Christ may be printed on small pieces of suede or flannel-backed construction paper. Pupils can take the pieces and place them in their correct positions on the flannel map. This same method and many variations may be used with maps of the wilderness wanderings, the divided kingdom, the journeys of Paul, and the mission fields of the world.

RELIEF MAPS

Three-dimensional maps can be made in several ways. A simple type of relief map can be made by using the sand table. Children and young people will gain profitable experiences from molding sand to represent mountains and other natural features of the terrain as they are found in the countries which are mentioned in the Bible. Strips of blue construction paper or mirrors will serve as bodies of water and rivers.

Another type of relief map can be made by using a cardboard or plywood base to construct a three-dimensional map from papier-mâché or plastic wood. Clay is also workable, but it is heavy and tends to crack. Plaster of paris used alone is not too workable since it dries rapidly and, as with clay, it is heavy.

A papier-mâché map may be easily prepared.

1. Make the outline of the map on a cardboard or plywood base.

2. Prepare the papier-mâché substance by cutting two-inch strips from a newspaper and soaking them in water for several hours. For good results, boil the substance for an hour or so and then let the paper soak overnight. Prepare a sufficient amount of paste made from flour and water and add a small amount of glue for better adhesiveness. Pour the water off the paper which has been soaking, and mix the paste substance with the paper.

3. Determine the approximate dimensions desired and carefully apply the papier-mâché to the cardboard, molding it with the hands. The vertical dimensions should be somewhat exaggerated over the horizontal so that they stand out. If exact proportions were used, mountains and hills would not be high enough to be noticeable. Do not move too rapidly. The job can be left at any time and continued later, providing certain areas are not left incomplete with oversized proportions that need to be changed.

4. Allow the freshly applied substance to dry thoroughly. Fill any holes with wood putty. If a smoother surface is desired, cover the map lightly with wall-paper paste or thick glue.

5. Finally, paint the map. Use blue poster paint to represent rivers and bodies of water. Other colors may be added as desired.

In addition to papier-mâché, another somewhat simpler idea has been presented by Marjorie East. The recipe is as follows:

> 1 pint ordinary sawdust
> 1 pint plaster
> 1 cup school library paste

Dissolve the paste in just enough water to thin lightly. Add plaster, then sawdust, and knead until the consistency is tough dough. Smooth onto model.[1]

ELECTRIC MAPS

Maps that are prepared with small light bulbs to indicate locations are extremely effective with all age groups. These bulbs, which can be lit with a dry-cell battery, may be added to a relief map. However, locations must be carefully thought through before papier-mâché or another substance is applied to the base. The best procedure is to leave holes and then to add the light fixtures after the substance dries.

Large wall maps can be prepared with light fixtures that can be operated by the teacher from a table or stand. Any amateur electrician in the church will be able to prepare maps of this type.

An outstanding accessory for every church is a large missionary map of

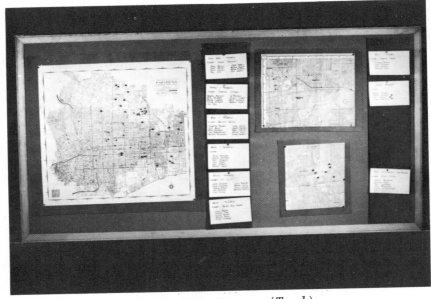

Fig. 41. Visitation map (*Teach*)

the world. Small lights which represent missionaries all over the world are very effective. These lights may be connected with the regular electrical current and operated with a single switch.

Every church should conduct a visitation program that reaches into the surrounding community. In most areas visitation maps are necessary to enable visitation teams to do an effective job. Various sized, up-to-date maps may be obtained for this purpose. By making inquiry at city halls or county seats, one can discover the sources of these maps.

In one growing community a map of the area was obtained for visitation purposes. Various-colored pins were placed on the map to indicate prospects, with each pin bearing a number which corresponded with a number on a card which contained the name and address of the new prospect. Several of these cards were placed in the hands of visitation teams on visitation night. If callers were not sure of certain locations, they were able to discover the exact routes and locations by viewing the map (see Fig. 41).

MAPS FOR TEACHING MISSIONS

The Great Commission is worldwide and it is virtually impossible to teach missions effectively without using maps. Beginning with school-age children, they may be used with all age levels (see Figs. 42-43).

GRAPHS

There are three basic types of graphs: line graphs, bar graphs, and circular or pie graphs.

LINE GRAPHS

Line graphs are very valuable in indicating changes. By comparing statistics and other facts, progress or decline can be graphically illustrated. For example, Sunday school attendance for a period of several years may be presented on a line graph as illustrated in Figure 44.

The horizontal lines represent the number of pupils attending Sunday school; the vertical lines represent the twelve months in the year. The solid, broken and dotted lines are used to represent three different years. In this Sunday school, marked progress is clearly evident.

Another subject which can be illustrated very well on a line graph is the amount of money received over a certain period. The offerings may be compared over a period of several years to show progress or decline just as illustrated with the attendance of a Sunday school. Another variation is to compare the amount received for the various funds of the church during a cer-

Fig. 42. Teaching worldwide missions (*Teach*)

Fig. 43. Teaching home missions (*Teach*)

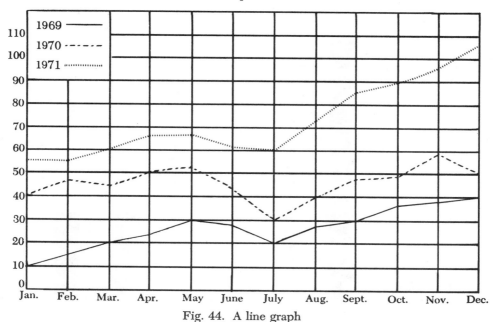

Fig. 44. A line graph

tain period of time. A solid line can represent the missionary fund, a broken line the general fund, and a dotted line the building fund. A final suggestion is to indicate with a single line the increase or decrease in the average monthly total over a certain period.

Line graphs may be used in a variety of ways. They are very effective visual aids for use in congregational meetings, Sunday school teachers' meetings, and board and committee meetings. With the proper explanation, they can present the truth vividly and concisely, and be much more effective in promoting and informing than are verbal presentations.

Line graphs should not be used alone on a bulletin board or poster unless they are very easy to read. Most graphs of this type require a certain amount of concentration and study in order to be understood by the observers. But a graph on a poster in the church lobby which is accompanied by a tape-recorded message is exceptionally attractive if the verbal explanation is presented clearly.

BAR GRAPHS

Bar graphs provide another means for presenting comparisons and changes. They are somewhat easier to read; they present more clearly information that deals with large numbers or other quantities. Statistics that illustrate church growth as compared with community growth are presented with the aid of two bar graphs in Figure 45.

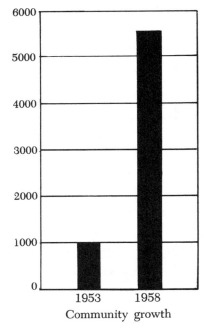
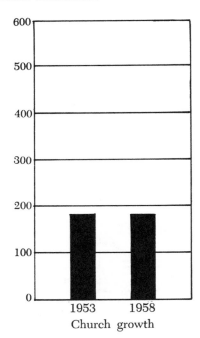

Fig. 45. Bar graphs

The horizontal lines indicate community growth in the graph on the left and church growth in the graph on the right. The two vertical bars in the graph at the left represent community population in 1953 and then in 1958; the two vertical bars in the graph at the right represent church membership also in 1953 and then in 1958. A quick glance reveals that in six years, while the community population has grown from 1,000 to 6,000, the church membership of 175 has remained the same. Two graphs such as these, placed on a bulletin board or in some other obvious place in the church, would clearly picture the great need for a concentrated effort to reach the people of the community for Christ.

CIRCULAR OR PIE GRAPHS

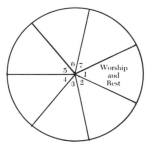

Pie graphs are very easy to make and to understand; simple ideas can even be understood by smaller children, which is not true of those presented on line and bar graphs. The total or whole is represented by a circle with each division indicating a certain part. This type of graph is illustrated in Figure 46.

Fig. 46. A pie graph

Since a circle may represent the total or whole of something, it may be used in a variety of ways. Teachers of older children, young people and adults can use pie or circular graphs extemporaneously and frequently on the chalkboard or drawing paper.

CHARTS

Charts may be used frequently to depict organizational plans and to show relationships. They aid greatly in giving an overall picture of a program, an idea, or a lesson.

ORGANIZATIONAL CHARTS

An organizational chart of a church program is given in Figure 47. It is easy to see that this church operates on a democratic basis; furthermore, it is unified. The elders and deacons are directly responsible to all members within the local church, while the pastor is responsible to both the church and the church board and is an advisory member on the board of elders and deacons and the board of Christian education. The board of Christian education is responsible to the elders and deacons and indirectly responsible to the church. This board is also responsible for bringing unity and balance to the various educational agencies of the church, which involve all ages. Charts such as this one may be used effectively in leadership training classes or in board or committee meetings to explain the overall educational work of the church.

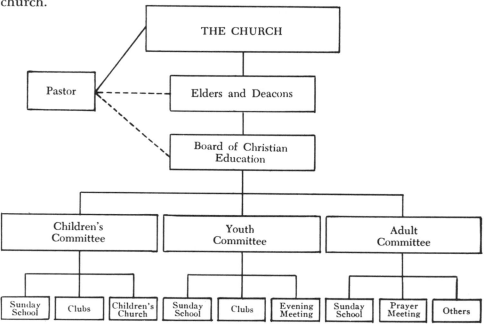

Fig. 47. An organizational chart

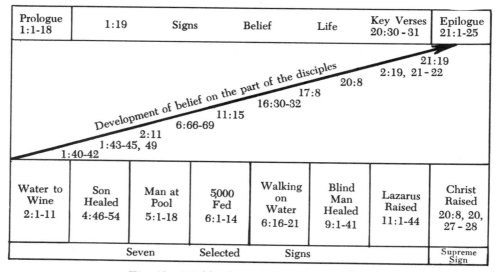

Fig. 48. A Bible chart of the gospel of John

BIBLE CHARTS

Charts may be prepared to aid in teaching the Bible. Biblical as well as other historical truths may be graphically illustrated with these visual aids. In Figure 48 the basic structure and content of an individual book of the Bible is shown. This chart can be easily enlarged, duplicated on 8½ x 11 inch sheets, and placed in the hands of each member of the class.

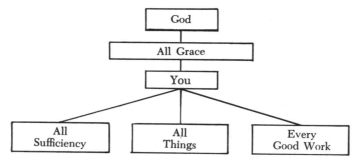

Fig. 49. A Bible chart of 2 Corinthians 9:8

Charts can be prepared for every book of the Bible and are particularly helpful in teaching survey courses where the teacher's goal is to give a quick overall view of each book. Well-prepared charts will stimulate thinking and pupil participation and will add variety to what may easily become a stereotyped method of teaching.

Charts may be used to illustrate a passage of Scripture or just one verse of the Bible. For example, 2 Corinthians 9:8 is illustrated in Figure 49.

A helpful chart which will greatly aid in individual or group Bible study is the "inductive Bible study chart" illustrated in Figure 50. This chart can be used by the individual in private Bible study or by the teacher as he leads his class in an inductive study of the Scriptures.

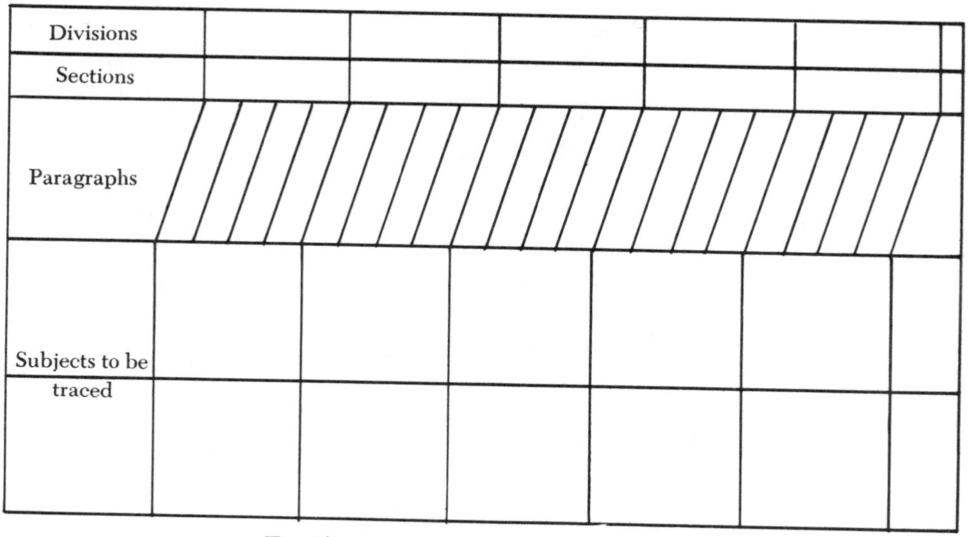

Fig. 50. An inductive Bible study chart

As the study continues, short titles or phrases illustrating the contents of each paragraph should be chosen and listed in the spaces indicated on the chart. Titles for the larger sections should be listed and, finally, the main divisions added. In addition, certain subjects can be traced through a book of the Bible at the same time the paragraph, section and division titles are formulated and listed.

When using the inductive chart in teaching, sections of the chart can be put on the chalkboard and developed by the class as the teacher leads the discussion. There will be, of course, much revision of the chart as it is formed, but this is part of the learning experience.

An inductive Bible study chart may become quite lengthy and detailed, but it is exceptionally helpful in determining the true structure of a book and the message that the author desired to convey. It also helps inspire people to think for themselves rather than to rely upon commentaries and other helps. In making such a study, one should use a modern English translation of the Bible which is organized into paragraphs. This will aid the student in choosing a key word or phrase which will summarize each paragraph.

Every Sunday school teacher should know how to use this method in

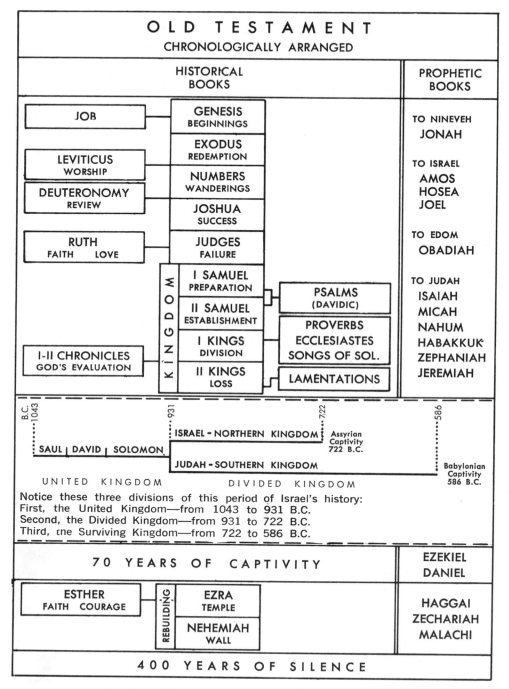

OLD TESTAMENT
CHRONOLOGICALLY ARRANGED

HISTORICAL BOOKS		PROPHETIC BOOKS

JOB — **GENESIS** BEGINNINGS

EXODUS REDEMPTION

LEVITICUS WORSHIP — **NUMBERS** WANDERINGS

DEUTERONOMY REVIEW — **JOSHUA** SUCCESS

RUTH FAITH LOVE — **JUDGES** FAILURE

KINGDOM:
I SAMUEL PREPARATION
II SAMUEL ESTABLISHMENT
I KINGS DIVISION
II KINGS LOSS

I-II CHRONICLES GOD'S EVALUATION

PSALMS (DAVIDIC)

PROVERBS ECCLESIASTES SONGS OF SOL.

LAMENTATIONS

PROPHETIC BOOKS:

TO NINEVEH **JONAH**

TO ISRAEL **AMOS HOSEA JOEL**

TO EDOM **OBADIAH**

TO JUDAH **ISAIAH MICAH NAHUM HABAKKUK ZEPHANIAH JEREMIAH**

B.C. 1043 ... 931 ... 722 ... 586

ISRAEL – NORTHERN KINGDOM   Assyrian Captivity 722 B.C.

SAUL | DAVID | SOLOMON

JUDAH – SOUTHERN KINGDOM   Babylonian Captivity 586 B.C.

UNITED KINGDOM   DIVIDED KINGDOM

Notice these three divisions of this period of Israel's history:
First, the United Kingdom—from 1043 to 931 B.C.
Second, the Divided Kingdom—from 931 to 722 B.C.
Third, the Surviving Kingdom—from 722 to 586 B.C.

70 YEARS OF CAPTIVITY   EZEKIEL DANIEL

ESTHER FAITH COURAGE — REBUILDING — EZRA TEMPLE / NEHEMIAH WALL

HAGGAI ZECHARIAH MALACHI

400 YEARS OF SILENCE

Fig. 51. Old Testament chronology chart (Hendricks)

GRID CHART

SOILS	KINDS	GROWTH	HINDRANCES	RESULTS
Wayside	Hard	Devoured—no growth	Birds Devil/Satan	Devoured
Stony	Shallow	Immediately sprang up— no deepness Germinated—no growth	Sun Not much earth Tribulation—persecution because of the Word	Scorched Withered
Thorny	Crowded	Choked Received/stumbled Some grow no fruit	Thorns Cares of the world Decline of rule Lust of other Christians	Yielded no fruit
Good	Receptive	Growing up Increasing Germinated—Growth— Varied fruitage	None Hears and accepts	Bear fruit 30/60/100 Different degrees

Fig. 52. Grid chart of four kinds of soil (Hendricks)

1b

Now it came to pass
   as I was

      —in Shusan the palace
      —in the 20th year
      —in the month of Chisleu

that Hanani . . . came
and I asked them

      —concerning the Jews
      —concerning Jerusalem

and they said unto me

      —the remnant . . . are in great affliction and reproach
      —the wall of Jerusalem . . . is broken down
      —and the gates thereof are burned with fire

3

4

And it came to pass
when I heard these words

                    —wept
                    —mourned   certain
that I sat down   —fasted   days
                    —prayed

Fig. 53. Grammatical chart (Hendricks)

private study. As each teacher prepares his lesson and is led by the Spirit of God, he will be able to bring to his pupils a fresh and vital message from the Scriptures.

Every Sunday school teacher should also know how to use this method in the classroom with young people and adults. A chart sketched on the chalkboard by the teacher as it is developed by the pupils will serve as a vital visual aid to help challenge thinking and make Bible study interesting and profitable (see Figs. 51-53 for additional Bible charts) .

Displaying Graphic Materials

Charts and graphs can be drawn or traced on poster board, drawing paper, newsprint, etc. They can also be effectively projected with an overhead projector (see Fig. 54) .

A turnover chart is easy to make. The drawn or written materials should be prepared on several sheets of durable paper and then the top edges of the sheets should be fastened to the top edge of a stand with a straight edge. After each page has been presented and discussed, it can be flipped over the top and back of the stand. A turnover chart may be used over and over again. In addition to displaying graphic materials, it may be used to teach songs, Scripture verses, to present outlines and to clarify many other ideas (see Fig. 55) .

Fig. 54. Projecting graphic material with the overhead projector (American Optical Corp.)

Fig. 55. Using a flip chart (*Teach*)

Discussion Questions

1. How could a missionary map of the world be used most effectively with a group of juniors (9-11)? With a group of young people or adults?

2. How could a map of Paul's missionary journeys be used to help teach the book of Philippians? First and Second Timothy?

Special Projects

1. Practice drawing freehand the maps which are given on pages 60 and 62. Be prepared to demonstrate to the group the effectiveness of being able to draw them extemporaneously on the chalkboard, a piece of drawing paper or on a piece of poster board.

2. Make a relief map from papier-mâché or some other workable substance.

3. Prepare a line, bar or circular graph on a large piece of poster board. Illustrate a subject in addition to those suggested in this chapter. Be prepared to demonstrate how the graph can be used.

4. On a piece of poster board or on some other suitable substance, prepare some type of organizational or Bible chart that is not already illustrated in this chapter. Strive toward originality. Be prepared to show the group how the chart can be used in teaching.

7

Visual Boards

CHALKBOARDS

CHALKBOARDS are one of the oldest visual techniques with unlimited opportunities for effective teaching. They can be utilized by any teacher or leader and used with all age groups for instruction, worship and expression. Charts, sketches, graphs, maps, memory verses, songs, outlines and announcements can be drawn or printed on the board to focus attention and to clarify ideas. Yet in many churches there are no chalkboards; in others, those at hand are infrequently used.

PURCHASING CHALKBOARDS

When purchasing these aids for the church, light-green boards with yellow chalk are preferable, for experiments have proved that this combination eases eye strain. However, other colors may be chosen to blend satisfactorily with the room furnishings. Black chalkboards are not suggested as they tend to make reading difficult and add to the gloomy atmosphere in rooms that already tend to be dark.

A certain number of portable chalkboards of different sizes should be purchased so that they can be removed from room to room and to different locations within a room. Permanent chalkboards placed on the walls are very helpful for use in small classrooms.

MAKING CHALKBOARDS

Excellent durable chalkboards can be made inexpensively from a piece of one-fourth-inch tempered masonite. The masonite can be cut into the desired size. A special green chalkboard surfacer which is made by several

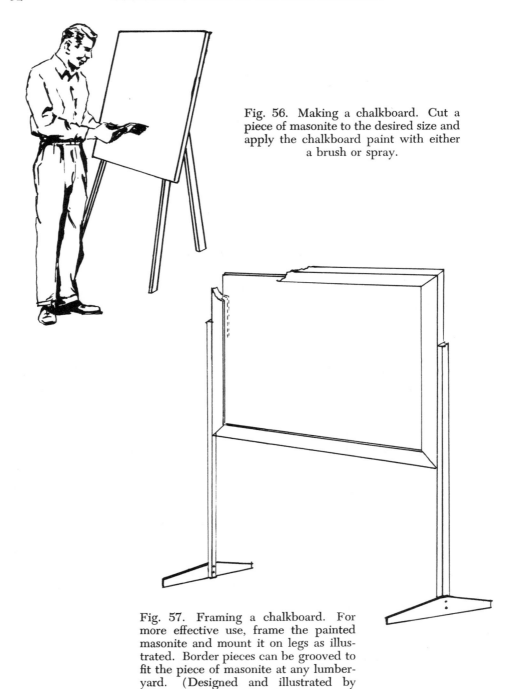

Fig. 56. Making a chalkboard. Cut a piece of masonite to the desired size and apply the chalkboard paint with either a brush or spray.

Fig. 57. Framing a chalkboard. For more effective use, frame the painted masonite and mount it on legs as illustrated. Border pieces can be grooved to fit the piece of masonite at any lumberyard. (Designed and illustrated by Loren Getz)

companies may be purchased and applied to the masonite. A wooden frame made for the chalkboard will add to its durability. Then, too, it is a simple matter to make legs for the chalkboard so it can be easily transported from place to place (see Figs. 56-57).

PRINCIPLES FOR USE

1. Think through beforehand what is to be printed or drawn on the chalkboard. This does not mean that unforeseen opportunities that will come during the session should not be used, but definite forethought is essential for effective utilization.

2. Write clearly and large enough so that all can see. Printing is preferable. Don't cram ideas together. Erase all irrelevant chalk marks by using smooth, downward strokes. Drawings and sketches should also be neat and clear.

3. Make sure that everyone can see. The chalkboard should be at the proper eye level and within arm's reach for the age group using it. Ordinarily, it is preferable to use the upper half of the board. Also check all areas of the room for glare. Stand to the side while writing so that what is being written or sketched can be seen.

4. Don't overuse the chalkboard to the exclusion of other visual techniques. For example, an extensive outline can be more easily duplicated and a copy given to each person rather than taking time to put it on the chalkboard, or it may be more effectively presented with an overhead projector.

TECHNIQUES FOR USE

1. Put large amounts of written work on the chalkboard before the class session begins.

2. Let pupils participate in writing or drawing (see Fig. 58).

3. Use the chalkboard to stimulate and direct class discussion. Write class contributions on the board and lead the group to formulate and outline a poem or a song, to develop other creative activities, or to arrive at conclusions to problems (see Fig. 59).

4. Use simple drawings such as stick figures to illustrate and explain (see chap. 8). Many times just a word or chalk mark will capture the wandering mind or help solve a discipline problem.

5. Use colored chalk to help gain attention and to add attractiveness.

6. Keep chalk from squeaking by holding it at a sharp angle.

7. Draw a straight line by marking two points. Place a piece of chalk on the first point. Keep your eyes focused on the second point and draw the line.

Fig. 58. Pupils participating in using a chalkboard (*Teach*)

Fig. 59. Using a chalkboard to stimulate and direct class discussion (*Teach*)

8. Draw a circle by placing the chalk at a point near the top of the chalkboard. Step back a comfortable arm's length and draw the circle rather quickly.

9. Use the perforated-paper method for more accurate drawings of maps and other sketches. Trace the pattern on a large sheet of drawing paper. Punch holes along the outlines of the drawing. Place the paper on the chalkboard and rub a chalky eraser over the holes several times. Remove the paper, and the outline of the drawing will be left on the chalkboard in the form of "dots." Fill in the outline with a piece of chalk.

10. Use the proportional-square method (see chap. 8). The enlarged squares, rather than being placed on a sheet of paper, should be placed on the chalkboard.

11. Use patterns cut from cardboard, wood, or another solid substance as templates for quickly tracing outlines on the chalkboard.

12. Make use of the suspense method. A series of drawings or written ideas can be placed on the chalkboard and then covered with a long sheet or roll of paper. One drawing at a time can be revealed as each is explained and discussed. This method creates interest. The orderly explanation also aids in clarifying ideas that may be complex and difficult to understand.

13. Use chalkboard wax to stick paper and cardboard materials on the chalkboard. This may be done without damage to the chalkboard. The wax may be purchased from school supply stores or audiovisual dealers.

BULLETIN BOARDS

Every church should have several bulletin boards placed in well-lighted, conspicuous places where notices, announcements, posters, clippings, cartoons, pictures, charts, creative work done by pupils, and other materials can be posted. They may be placed on walls, hung from ceilings, or placed on easels in church lobbies, hallways, stairlandings, and in class and departmental rooms (see Fig. 60).

Bulletin boards can be all sizes, but each one should be large enough to serve its particular purpose. Most boards should never be less than three to four feet in height. If desired, they may even be the width of an entire wall.

<table>
<tr><td>Fig. 60. Bulletin boards can serve as a motivational tool (Teach)</td><td>Fig. 61. Here an inexpensive composition material is used to make a bulletin board on the backside of a piano (Teach)</td></tr>
</table>

Bulletin boards may be purchased or made. A cork material is considered to be best, but it is more expensive than other substances. Excellent inexpensive bulletin boards can be made from composition materials such as celotex (see Fig. 61).

TYPES

Many different types of bulletin boards can be prepared and used in the church. Another possibility is the use of one large board with various divisions.

Pastor's bulletin board. Every pastor should have his own bulletin board. It may be prepared and kept in order by himself or his secretary. From his weekly reading he will discover outstanding articles, quotations and cartoons that should be brought to the attention of his congregation. From this correspondence he will receive letters and announcements that should be posted. He will want to post his own personal prayer requests as well as those received from others in the congregation which are not confidential. He should keep his people informed of coming messages and of special board, committee, prayer and congregational meetings.

Missionary bulletin board. One excellent way for the missionary committee to keep the missionary activities of the church before the congregation is by means of a missionary bulletin board. Prayer cards from all missionaries supported by the church should be posted on this board. Missionary letters with key sentences and phrases underlined along with up-to-date photographs taken on the field should be used. Missionary prayer requests should be listed in an orderly manner, and special missionary prayer meetings in the church should be announced. In addition, a different field or an individual missionary or missionary couple may be featured each month with pertinent information regarding progress, special blessings, and problems on the field.

Sunday school bulletin board. Since the Sunday school is the largest and most important agency in the average church, its activities must be kept before the people. Charts and graphs indicating growth or decline in attendance may be posted to aid in promoting the work of the Sunday school. Statistics of community growth as compared with the progress in reaching the people of the community tend to awaken the church to its responsibility. Articles from periodicals dealing with the ministry of the Sunday school, tips for teachers, and book reviews provide helpful information. Future plans for Sunday school teachers' and officers' conferences and other regular activities should be kept before all Sunday school workers. An additional sidelight on the Sunday school bulletin board is the superintendent's corner where he can post prayer requests, squibs, special announcements and cartoons.

Young people's bulletin board. Youth groups, too, need to publicize their activities. On the young people's bulletin board, which should be prepared and kept up-to-date by the young people themselves, may be posted photographs taken at youth activities, good book reviews, newspaper and magazine clippings, charts and graphs indicating growth or decline in attendance, posters publicizing coming events, announcements of gospel team meetings, information about outstanding Bible schools and colleges, humorous and serious cartoons, prayer requests, and challenging quotations and squibs regarding Bible study, prayer, witnessing, and the like.

Church music bulletin board. Every church with an active musical program needs a bulletin board to announce special musical programs and to keep choir members informed regarding special rehearsals, socials, prayer meetings and prayer requests. The names of those who have been asked to sing solos and to perform in special musical groups should be posted with the specific dates and the time of the meetings.

Departmental or classroom bulletin board. All of the bulletin boards mentioned previously serve primarily as a means to inform and publicize. A bulletin board in a departmental room or classroom will serve primarily as an aid in teaching. Flat pictures, especially, as they are used with children to clarify and summarize weekly lessons, should be placed on the bulletin board to provide opportunity for review and to aid in applying Christian truth to the pupils' lives. Creative work done by pupils, such as drawings, poems, songs and stories, should be posted for all to see. Older groups will appreciate magazine and newspaper articles and pictures that are directly related to their units of study.

Christian education bulletin board. A Christian education bulletin board, planned and prepared by the Christian education board or committee, will serve as an excellent visual aid to interest the church as a whole in Christian education activities. Since one of the goals of this committee or board is to bring unity into the church program, this unique opportunity should be seriously considered.

The following list is prepared to give ideas for featuring leadership personnel, organizations, agencies, and activities throughout the church year. As is clearly evident, one theme such as "leadership" may be featured for several months or even longer. Rather than changing the bulletin board each week, it may be desirable to leave it for two weeks so that everybody will have an opportunity to notice it. The ideas may be worked out as bulletin board displays by the use of photographs, printed Scripture texts, lists of responsibilities, prayer requests, needs, activities, goals, statistics, etc.

1. Leadership
   a. Pastor and family
   b. Board of elders
   c. Board of deacons
   d. Assistant pastor
   e. Director of Christian education
   f. Christian education committee or board
   g. Choir director
   h. Sunday school superintendent and the executive staff (assistant, secretary and treasurer)
   i. Other committee chairmen and members
2. Sunday school[1]
   a. Nursery department

     b. Kindergarten department

     c. Primary department

     d. Junior department

     e. Junior high department

     f. Senior department

     g. Young people's department

     h. Young married people's class

     i. Adult classes

     j. Leadership training class

3. Clubs

     a. Girls

     b. Boys

4. Music

     a. Adult choir

     b. Youth choir

     c. Children's choir

     d. Special (soloists, duets, quartets, etc.)

5. Vacation Bible school

     a. Departments

        (1) Nursery and kindergarten

        (2) Primary and junior

        (3) Junior high and other youth classes

        (4) Adult classes and leadership

     b. Activities

        (1) Stories and songs

        (2) Worship

        (3) Refreshments and recreation

        (4) Handcraft

6. Missions (see section entitled *Missionary bulletin board*)

7. Prayer groups

     a. Midweek

     b. Missionary

8. Youth organizations

     a. Junior highs

     b. Seniors

     c. Young people

9. Weekday church school

10. Church nursery

11. Children's church

12. Junior church

13. Gospel teams

14. Sunday school teachers' and officers' conferences
15. Sunday morning service
16. Sunday evening service
17. Midweek Bible study

In addition to the list of ideas just presented, there are special days and weeks which can be periodically the subjects for the Christian education bulletin board.

1. National Youth Week
2. Palm Sunday
3. Easter
4. National Family Week
5. Mother's Day
6. Pentecost
7. Children's Day
8. Father's Day
9. Rally Day
10. Christian Education Sunday
11. National Sunday School Week
12. World Wide Communion Sunday
13. Christian Home Sunday
14. Veterans' Day (Armistice Day)
15. Thanksgiving
16. Universal Bible Sunday
17. Christmas

Fig. 62. Bulletin boards should be eye level (*Teach*)

Fig. 63. Keep bulletin boards up-to-date (*Teach*)

Changeable-letter bulletin board. An attractive changeable-letter bulletin board placed on the church lawn or in the church lobby is very helpful in publicizing special events and the various services of the church. Both indoor and outdoor types are available. The letters may be changed quickly and easily. A special board may also be obtained with electric bulbs that are properly placed to illuminate the whole board and the name of the church.

Fig. 64. Using 3-D effects (*Teach*)

Fig. 65. Using bulletin boards to promote group projects (*Teach*)

PRINCIPLES AND SUGGESTIONS FOR USE

1. Place bulletin boards where they can be easily seen. If they are located in department rooms, they should be at eye level and within arms' reach of all pupils (see Fig. 62).

2. Keep bulletin boards up-to-date. Don't allow them to become cluttered with antiquated materials (see Fig. 63).

3. Make bulletin board displays interesting and attractive. Prepare three-dimensional effects by using an adhesive such as wax to fasten objects to bulletin boards. With a little thought, ingenious ideas can be used. Movement always aids greatly in attracting attention (see Fig. 64).

4. Use bulletin boards to promote group projects. Teachers should give guidance but should let the pupils be responsible for planning and preparing the materials. The amount of supervision will be governed by the age group (see Fig. 65).

5. Give guidance in bulletin board preparation. Conduct a special meeting for those who are responsible for bulletin board planning in order to

give suggestions regarding effective composition. Subjects such as a center of interest, captions and legends, clarity, simplicity, color and variety may be discussed.

FLANNELBOARDS

Christian workers have made use of flannelboards for many years, and these vital visual tools have aided greatly in helping to bring many to a saving knowledge of Christ and to growth in grace. Bible stories, object lessons, memory work, map studies, biographies and missions have been presented interestingly, visually and effectively with all age groups.

Flannelboard materials are known by a variety of names. They have been called flannelgraphs, slap boards, magic boards, story-o-graphs, gospel-graphs, mission-graphs, suede-o-graphs, felt-o-graphs, etc. All of these names apply to pieces of substantial, light-weight materials such as plywood, celotex, masonite, bristol board, wallboard or heavy cardboard which have been covered with flannel or other soft, napped fabric. Felt is also used as a covering but is considerably more expensive. Pictures, symbols, letters and other objects are also backed with flannel, suede paper or felt. Since these materials will adhere to each other, the figures and objects can be placed on the flannelboard as a story or other message is presented.

Flannelboard equipment and materials can either be purchased from commercial sources or they can be easily made.

COMMERCIALLY MADE EQUIPMENT AND MATERIALS

Flannelboards. Flannelboards may be purchased from Christian bookstores as well as from school supply stores. A common size is 24 x 36 inches. When purchasing a flannelboard, select one that is sturdy, light-weight, and one that will fold in the middle to permit easy handling and storage.

Stands or easels. Either wooden or light-weight metal flannelboard stands may be purchased from the same sources as flannelboards. Both are reasonably priced, although metal stands are usually more expensive.

When purchasing a stand, select one that can be easily adjusted for different heights. This is necessary to make it usable with all age groups. Also select one that can be folded or collapsed and stored in a small convenient container. This will enable one to transport it easily from place to place and to store it conveniently without taking up too much space.

Backgrounds. Colorful flannel or felt background scenes may be purchased for use on flannelboards. An attractive Palestine landscape with Judean hills and a beautifully painted sky will help make Bible stories live for children. Various scenes may be bought: a street, a desert, a seashore, a general outdoor scene, an interior scene, etc.

Oil-painted backgrounds are usually the best buy but are more expensive than those prepared with water colors or chalk. When purchasing, consider the artistic quality and avoid gaudy backgrounds that will detract from the flannelboard figures and the message.

Flannelboard scenes that may be colored by teachers also are available. Many of the same scenes mentioned above are available on white flannel, ready to be colored with chalk, crayons or paint. Sketchos, which are oil colors in stick form, will do an effective job.

Flannelboard maps are excellent for teaching Bible geography. The exodus, the wilderness wanderings, the life of Christ, and Paul's missionary journeys can be graphically presented with these colorful visual aids. Suede-backed symbols, which accompany some of these maps, are helpful in aiding pupils to visualize geographical locations.

Figures and objects. A variety of flannelboard figures or cutouts are available from Christian publishers and bookstores. Written materials which describe the lessons and illustrate how to use them and make backgrounds for them usually accompany these figures and objects. Built-up Bible stories which dramatically present the story of creation, the stories of Noah, Moses, David, Elijah, the life of Christ, the life of Paul and others are exceptionally appealing to children. Most of the figures are beautifully colored, or they may be colored by the teachers. Many are backed with suede and are easily prepared for use (see Fig. 66).

Especially prepared cutouts are also available to aid pupils in memorizing Scripture verses, entire passages, songs, the books of the Bible, etc. These aids are particularly helpful in making memory work interesting, meaningful and applicable to life experiences.

Fig. 66. Examples of flannelgraph materials (Scripture Press)

Exceptionally interesting missionary stories, character stories, and object lessons are also available. Young people will enjoy biblical themes which have been graphically prepared and illustrated, such as the fruit of the Spirit, the Christian's two natures and Christian living.

MAKING FLANNELBOARD EQUIPMENT AND MATERIALS

Frequently churches have members who are carpenters or machinists and own their own tools for doing professional work. These men can make flannelboards and stands that are just as durable and usable as those made commercially. Much money can be saved by these workers who consider the opportunity to prepare this equipment as an occasion to serve the Lord. Then, too, there are simple ideas that can be worked out by people without professional abilities.

Flannelboards. An excellent flannelboard may be prepared by using plywood, celotex, masonite, bristol board, wallboard or heavy cardboard. These materials are satisfactory in that they will not warp. It is a simple matter to cut any one of these materials to the desired size and then to cover the piece with flannel or other soft, napped fabric. The cloth may be fastened to the board with staples, brads, binding tape or thumbtacks. If the piece of flannel is large enough, it can be prepared to cover both sides of the board. Three sides of the piece of flannel should be sewed together to form a pillow-case effect. The board can be easily slipped into the flannel covering, and the fourth side sewed by hand.

Plywood will serve as an excellent backing material for making a more professional type of flannelboard. Figure 67 illustrates how to make one that will fold in the middle for easy handling and storage. The following steps will aid in the preparation of this flannelboard:

1. Cut a piece of one-quarter-inch plywood so that it will measure 24 x 36 inches. Cut this piece in half so that each piece measures 18 x 24 inches.

2. Lay the two pieces on a flat surface and fasten them together with small butt hinges which may be purchased from any hardware store. Place the hinges so that when the two pieces are folded together, the hinges are on the inside (see diagram).

3. Apply the flannel to each half of the folding board on the outer surface so that the hinges will not be in the way.

Another convenient type of flannelboard is one that can be set on the top of a table. Figure 68 illustrates how to make this type. The following steps will aid in its preparation:

1. Cut a piece of one-quarter-inch plywood so that it will measure 24 x 36 inches.

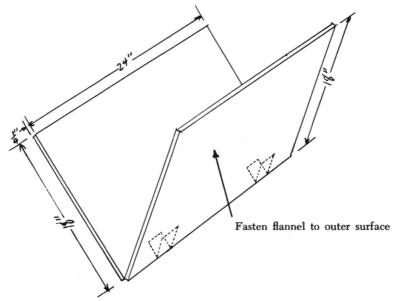

Fasten flannel to outer surface

Fig. 67. A folding flannelboard

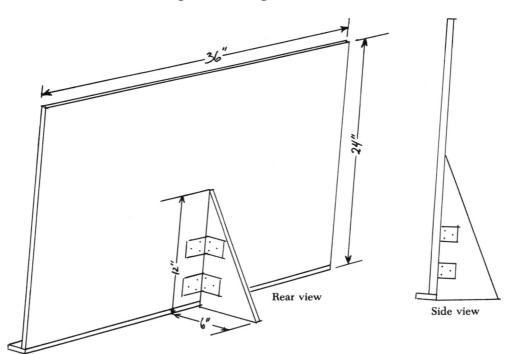

Rear view

Side view

Fig. 68. A table-model flannelboard and stand

2. Cut a narrow strip of plywood 36 inches long and 1 inch wide and fasten it to the bottom edge of the board to form a small ledge. This will allow the board to be used as a regular flannelboard stand, a stand for small chalkboards, posters, charts, pictures and other visual aids.

3. Cut a leg or support 12 inches long and 6 inches wide at the base. Make sure the base is cut slightly less than a 90 degree angle (see diagram for side view), which will allow the stand to lean back at a slight angle so that figures and other flannelboard objects will more easily adhere to the board. Fasten the leg to the stand with small butt hinges which may be purchased at any hardware store.

4. Apply the piece of flannel to the face of the board. If desired, the piece of flannel need not be fastened permanently to the board but merely tacked to the top edge. This will enable teachers to remove the flannel when the stand is to be used for other purposes.

Stands or easels. Two types of stands or easels may be made. The first type can be constructed from electrical thin-wall conduit or other kinds of metal tubing. The second type can be made from good quality lumber.

Metal stands. Metal stands are the most durable, but they are more complicated to construct than those made from wood. However, metal stands can be made by any person who knows how to use a drill, a hacksaw and a vise. Purchase the following materials:

1. Six pieces of electrical thin-wall conduit 32 inches long, from any electrical shop, lumberyard or hardware store.

2. One piece of fourteen-gauge sheet metal approximately 6 x 6 inches from any sheet metal shop.

3. Fourteen 3/16 x 1-inch roundheaded stove bolts.

The following instructions will aid in the preparation of the easel (see figure 69):

1. Cut the side plates (A) for the leg joints from the piece of fourteen-gauge sheet metal. Round off the edges on an electric grinder for a neater job.

2. Use a 3/16-inch drill (drill press if possible) to make the holes in the tubing and through the side plates to form the leg joints. Notice that a single bolt in the top section of the leg forms the hinge.

3. Cut the bracket (B) and the top crosspiece (C) from the fourteen-gauge sheet metal according to the dimensions given in Figure 69. Use a vise to form the U-shaped bracket for the rear leg. Center the bracket on the crosspiece and either bolt or weld the pieces together. The next step is to bolt the two front legs to the top crosspiece and the rear leg to the U-shaped bracket.

4. Place a rubber tip on each leg. The stand is self-supporting and will

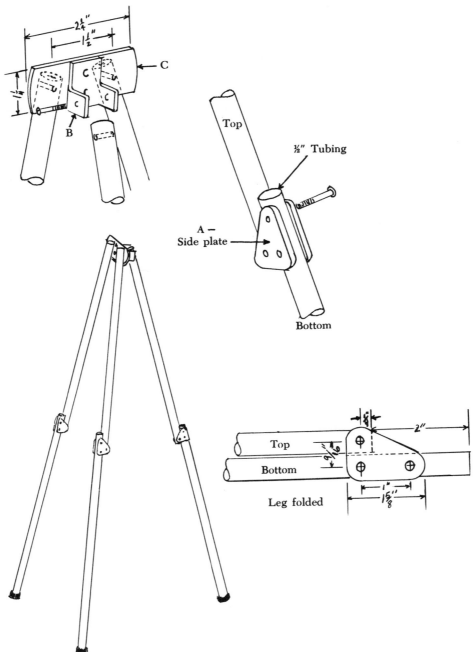

Fig. 69. A metal folding easel (designed and illustrated by Loren Getz)

not slip due to the rubber tips. The flannelboard may be placed on the two ledges formed by the front leg joints or, if desired, small adjustable hooks may be added. When the stand is not in use, it may be folded into one compact unit for easy handling and storage.

A simpler stand may also be made by using the same principles illustrated in Figure 69. Instead of purchasing six pieces of conduit 32 inches long, purchase three pieces 64 inches long. The only work necessary is to make the top crosspiece and the U-joint to add hooks to the legs to hold the flannelboard. The stand, of course, will not fold, but it may be placed in a corner of a room or in a closet.

Wooden stands. Various ideas can be used to construct wooden easels. The stand that is presented in Figure 70 illustrates one of the simplest types. It can be constructed quickly by any person who can handle a few tools.

Purchase the following materials:

a. three pieces of lumber 1 x 2 x 66 inches

b. two pieces of lumber 1 x 2 x 24 inches

c. one piece of lumber 1 x 4 x 6 inches

d. one 3-inch T-hinge

e. two small chains 12 to 14 inches in length

f. six ¼ x 1¾-inch carriage bolts (two of the bolts should have wing nuts)

g. four ¼ x 1-inch carriage bolts

Instructions for building the stand are as follows:

1. Lay two of the 1 x 2 x 66-inch leg pieces together (clamp together or place in a vise). Drill the desired number of holes for the adjustable crosspiece (B) with a 5/16-inch drill bit.

2. Cut crosspiece (A) at the desired angles to give the proper leg spread. Bolt the two front legs to this piece with four of the ¼ x 1¾-inch carriage bolts.

3. Bolt the hinge to the rear leg and crosspiece (A) with the four ¼ x 1-inch carriage bolts.

4. Fasten the chains with three large staples.

5. Use the two pieces of lumber 1 x 2 x 24 inches to prepare crosspiece (B). Nail or screw them together and place the completed piece in an inverted position on the stand so it will lie flat against the two front legs. Use the two ¼ x 1¾-inch carriage bolts with the wing nuts to fasten this piece to the stand. It can be adjusted for various heights.

Another easily constructed wooden stand, presented in Figure 71, has certain advantages over the stand in Figure 70 in that it can be folded into a more compact unit. The crossbar can be removed and the legs folded together as illustrated in the enlarged drawing.

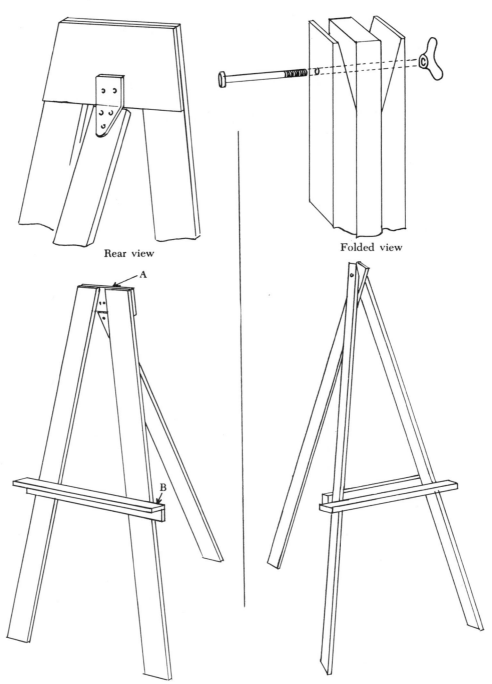

Rear view

Folded view

Fig. 70. A wooden semifolding easel

Fig. 71. A wooden folding easel

Purchase the following materials:

a. Three pieces of lumber 1 x 2 x 66 inches.

b. Two pieces of lumber 1 x 4 x 24 inches.

c. One ¼ x 2½-inch carriage bolt with a wing nut.

d. One ¼ x 4-inch carriage bolt with a wing nut.

1. Lay the three leg pieces together and drill a hole near the top of each one. Cut the proper angles on the top of the two outside legs as illustrated in the enlarged drawing in Figure 71. Fasten them together with the ¼ x 2½-inch carriage bolt.

2. Make the crosspiece from the two ¼ x 4 x 24-inch pieces of lumber. Place the front ledge edgeways against the front side of the legs; place the rear piece with the broad surface against the backside of the legs. Drill a hole through the middle of both pieces. Use the ¼ x 4-inch carriage bolt to hold them together.

3. Tighten the wing nut at the top of the easel when the stand is set up, which will keep the stand from collapsing. To keep the legs from slipping, tack a small piece of rubber to the bottom of each leg.

Backgrounds. Two types of easily prepared flannelboard backgrounds are built-up and solid backgrounds.

Built-up backgrounds. The built-up backgrounds of outdoor scenes are prepared from various pieces of colored flannel which are cut to represent mountains, roads, trees, water, grass, bushes, etc. The scenes are built up directly on the flannelboard. The following steps will enable any Christian worker to prepare and use attractive background scenes:

1. Notice the scene in Figure 72. This is a basic outdoor scene which may be used just as it is for a number of Bible and missionary stories.[2] The additional scenes in Figures 73-77 are variations of this basic scene to which additional details have been added, such as trees, a road, bushes, water, etc. Any one of these six scenes may be prepared first, but it is necessary to refer always to scene number one for the basic dimensions.

2. After selecting the scene desired, prepare a full-sized 24 x 36-inch paper background before attempting to prepare a scene in its final form from flannel pieces. Ordinary newsprint or wrapping paper may be used for this purpose.

3. Sketch in the outlines of the particular scene that has been chosen with a dark pencil or crayon. Be sure to follow the dimensional instructions given in Figure 72. Experiment until the right proportions are determined. For more accurate work, use the opaque projector, an overhead projector, or the pantograph.

4. Buy a number of different-colored pieces of flannel to represent the necessary details as illustrated in Figures 72-77. Although a number of differ-

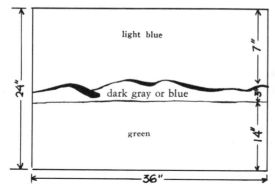

Fig. 72. A built-up background, scene 1

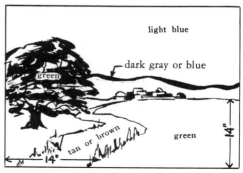

Fig. 73. A built-up background, scene 2

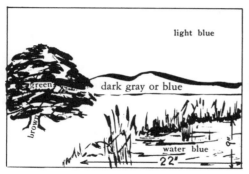

Fig. 74. A built-up background, scene 3

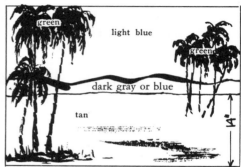

Fig. 75. A built-up background, scene 4

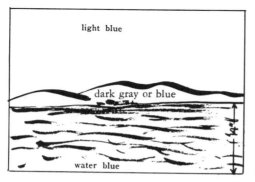

Fig. 76. A built-up background, scene 5

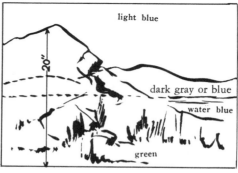

Fig. 77. A built-up background, scene 6

ent colors are available, the following will be satisfactory for the preparation of all six scenes: (1) light blue for the sky, (2) dark gray or blue for the mountains, (3) green for the landscape, tree leaves, bushes, etc., (4) tan or brown for the road piece and tree trunks, and (5) water blue for bodies of water.

5. Cut the various sections from the paper sample and pin them to the appropriate pieces of colored flannel to serve as patterns. It is now a simple matter to cut the flannel pieces the correct size.

6. Save all the scraps of flannel that are left after the main cutting process is finished. Use these small pieces to make trees, bushes, rocks, and to add other interesting details.

7. Add additional colors to pieces of flannel by using colored chalk, colored pencils, wax crayons, Sketchos, textile paints, oil paints or poster paints.

It is advisable to use built-up backgrounds indoors. A slight gust of wind will easily remove them unless they are in some way fastened securely to the flannelboard. When using them indoors there will be no problems if the flannelboard is set at a slight angle.

Solid backgrounds. Various indoor and outdoor solid background scenes may be prepared on white or light-colored flannel. Solid backgrounds are similar to those made commercially. One scene is prepared on each 24 x 36-inch piece of flannel with the aid of colored pieces of chalk, colored pencils, wax crayons, Sketchos, textile paints, oil paints or poster paints. Colored chalk is one of the easiest means of preparing colorful backgrounds as it can be applied very smoothly and quickly. However, colored chalk smudges very easily unless the scene is sprayed periodically with a fixative. Colored pencils used with water also work well, but the process takes longer. Wax crayons are advantageous in that the completed backgrounds may be pressed with a hot iron to make them color fast. Sketchos do an excellent job, but they are harder to blend; they, too, must be sprayed with a fixative to keep them from smudging. Paints do a more professional job, provided they are used by a professional hand. All of these mediums will enable one to do good work; but no matter which is used, all backgrounds should be folded in tissue paper when they are stored.

Figures and objects. Most Christian workers prefer to buy flannelboard figures and objects even though they may desire to make the other equipment and materials. Yet there are many types of figures and objects that may be prepared. Printed materials are very helpful, especially with older children, young people and adults. They may be prepared by printing Scripture references, words, etc., on strips of construction paper and then backing them with sandpaper, felt, flannel, suede paper or blotter paper. If the construction paper is rough enough, it will adhere to flannel without additional backing.

In addition, objects may be cut from construction paper and prepared in the same manner. Pictures cut from magazines and from other sources are very effective. Children will enjoy preparing their own materials; young people and adults can help to prepare them for use with the younger age groups.

PRINCIPLES FOR USE

1. Do not overuse the flannelboard. This is a major problem among many Christian workers. Due to this abuse, in many situations the attention of pupils is no longer held by the novelty of the flannelboard. If this is the case, it needs to be laid aside for a time while other visual techniques are used.

2. Do not allow the use of the flannelboard to be a substitute for preparation. Study the lesson thoroughly and practice using the flannelboard before presenting the lesson.

3. Make sure all flannelboard figures are in their proper order for use before the class or worship service begins.

4. Make sure the flannelboard is resting at a slight angle. This will help backgrounds and figures to adhere to the flannelboard and is especially necessary when built-up backgrounds are used.

5. Tack or clip the pieces of flannel to the top of the board if more than one solid background is being used, so that each scene can be folded over the top and back of the flannelboard.

6. Make sure that all can see. Adjust the easel so that the board is at the proper level. Stand to the side as the story is told.

7. Do not confuse children by interchanging figures. Children will recognize a figure that was used to represent John in one scene and Peter in the next scene.

8. Keep cutouts from each lesson in file folders or envelopes and filed in good order. Mark every piece in each set so each one can be identified if misplaced. If certain figures are used and adapted for stories different from the original, make sure that they get back to the original set.

TECHNIQUES FOR USE

1. Periodically, let the children tell the story and manipulate the figures. This is a good test of whether they have grasped the meaning of the story and also allows for pupil participation (see Fig. 78) .

2. To add variety, record the lesson on tape. Very interesting sound effects and a musical background may also be added.

3. Let children create an original flannelboard story for a special program such as Easter, Christmas, or for a vacation Bible school demonstration night. Pictures may be cut from magazines and other sources and backed

Fig. 78. Pupils participating in the use of a flannelboard (Standard Publishing)

Fig. 79. Building up a concept or idea on a flannelboard (*Teach*)

with flannel. A story can be written by the group and recorded on tape with other background effects. This will, of course, require much close supervision, but children will thoroughly enjoy preparing the project and will be doubly thrilled as it is presented.

4. Use Bible story records and other types with the flannelboard. It will be necessary to prepare the flannelboard presentations to fit the messages on the records since records are not specifically prepared for this purpose.

5. Don't forget the possibilities for using the flannelboard with adults. Captions, outlines, and pictorial illustrations can be very effective (see Fig. 79).

Discussion Questions

1. What suggestions can be offered for keeping a church bulletin board in good order?

2. How can teachers and other workers be motivated to make greater use of the chalkboard?

3. What suggestions can be given for keeping flannel board materials filed and in good order?

Special Projects

1. Make a chalkboard, using a piece of tempered masonite and chalkboard paint. If possible, put a frame around the masonite and mount it on legs.

2. Be prepared to demonstrate before the group the various chalkboard techniques mentioned in this chapter.

3. Make a bulletin board from some type of composition material and prepare some type of bulletin board display. (If materials are not available to make a bulletin board, draw a bulletin board on a sheet of paper; by means of diagrams, illustrate some type of display.)

4. Be prepared to demonstrate before the group a well-told flannelboard story, using commercially prepared figures.

5. Construct a simple flannelboard and stand from the instructions given in this chapter.

6. Prepare the build-up background materials illustrated in this chapter. Demonstrate the use of these materials before the group.

7. Prepare an original flannelboard lesson, using your own figures, objects, word cards, etc. Demonstrate before the group how it can be used.

8

Nonprojected Still Pictures

DRAWINGS

BRUCE MCINTYRE, as quoted in the *Manual of Audio-Visual Techniques,* has stated: "More important to society than the teaching of drawing as a subject of art, is the teaching of drawing as a means of communicating visual knowledge."[1]

When the word *church* is substituted for the word *society,* this quotation is directly applicable to the ministry of Christian education. Christian workers who use simple drawings and sketches to make their teaching clear have discovered a valuable means of aiding communication. A simple sketch of a stick figure associated with an idea can focus attention, clarify that idea, and add variety to the teaching-learning process.

FREEHAND DRAWING

Both teachers and pupils can learn to draw simple sketches (see Fig. 80). Drawings that are made to teach concepts do not stand by themselves as pieces of art, but are associated with the subject matter being discussed. They are used primarily to represent a thing or an idea rather than to repro-

Fig. 80. Using simple drawing to illustrate a basic Christian truth (*Teach*)

Fig. 81. Freehand drawings

duce professionally a sketch of a person or an object. A little practice will give any teacher a repertoire of ideas for illustrating with simple drawings. For example, the simple figures illustrated in Figure 81 can be used to aid in communicating various ideas for all age groups.

TECHNIQUES FOR DRAWING

In addition to simple freehand sketches that can be used by every teacher, several techniques may be used to reproduce more complicated drawings.

Opaque projector. The opaque projector enables Christian workers to project almost any picture or drawing onto the chalkboard, a sheet of drawing paper, a sheet of poster board or a piece of flannel. The image may be made the desired size by moving the projector closer or farther from the drawing surface. It is then a simple matter to trace the picture with chalk, crayon, a drawing pencil or a felt-tipped pen. Any unnecessary details may be omitted.

All teachers who have access to an opaque projector can prepare excellent drawings ahead of time for use in the classroom. This method of drawing will work well with all types of pictures, maps and sketches, provided the original copies are small enough to fit into the projector. To be able to set up the projector and to trace the image as it is projected are the only skills needed.

Fig. 82. Using the opaque projector (Charles Beseler Co.)

Originally, of course, the opaque projector was *not* designed for drawing and tracing purposes but was developed so that pictures, graphics and textual material could be projected on the screen. Even small objects and specimens, such as a watch, a piece of rock, a missionary curio, etc., provided they are not too thick, can be projected (see Fig. 82).

The problem with the opaque projector, however, is that it takes a completely darkened room. Furthermore, many drawings, and especially written materials, contain print so small it is impossible to read it on the screen at any distance.

Unless there are special reasons and purposes, such an extensive drawing, for using the opaque projector, it is not recommended as a primary investment. Furthermore, the overhead projector allows you to do almost everything you can do with the opaque, and you can do it much more effectively.

The pantograph. The pantograph, an inexpensive instrument that may be purchased from an art supply store, can be used to enlarge or reduce the size of drawings accurately and quickly. The pantograph should be fastened securely to a table (see Fig. 83). As the first pointer is moved along the outlines of the original drawing, the second pointer will reproduce the sketch in the desired size which is dependent on the adjustment of the instrument.

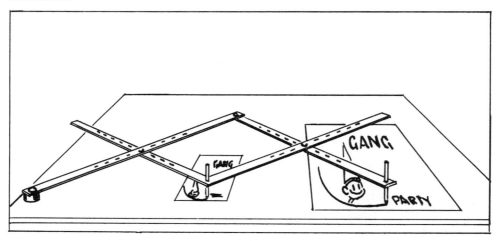

Fig. 83. Using the pantograph

Proportional squares. Drawings may also be easily enlarged by using the proportional-square method. Squares are made directly on the original drawing, or the drawing may be traced on another sheet of paper and then prepared with squares. An extended diagonal line will help determine the desired size of the reproduction. When proportional squares are drawn on the larger copy, the original may be copied square for square as illustrated in Figure 84.

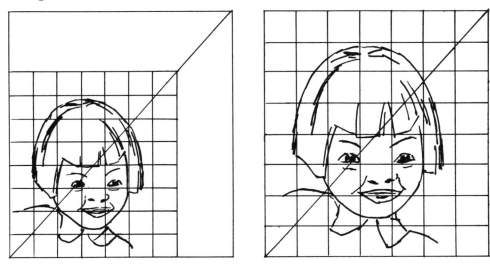

Fig. 84. Using proportional squares

FLAT PICTURES

Flat pictures for use in Christian education are of two types: those prepared commercially for specific use in the church, and those that come from other sources. Both types are valuable as visual aids.

PICTURES PREPARED COMMERCIALLY

Publishing houses that specialize in printing curriculum materials for use in the church usually prepare teaching pictures to accompany their materials (see Fig. 85). These pictures are prepared particularly for use in curriculum units to aid in teaching biblical truths and to lead pupils into worship experiences. Additional flat pictures may also be obtained from publishers who specialize in preparing teaching pictures. These commercially made prints are invaluable in helping teachers to accomplish the goals of Christian education.

OTHER SOURCES

Pictures that have not been prepared particularly for commercial purposes may be obtained from many sources. They may be clipped from magazines, books, pamphlets, newspapers, calendars, quarterlies, Sunday school papers, catalogs, and travel circulars, or they may be in the form of postcards, Christmas, Easter and other special-day cards. Selected carefully,

Fig. 85. Bible-teaching picture set (Scripture Press)

Fig. 86. Using pictures from many sources (*Teach*)

they can provide an inexpensive but priceless source of pictures for use in all areas of the church (see Fig. 86).

CRITERIA FOR SELECTION

It is important to select good pictures. The following criteria will aid in selecting both commercially made pictures and pictures from other sources:

1. Will the pictures make a real contribution in helping to achieve the goals of Christian education?

2. Are the pictures truthful?

   a. Will the pupils gain wrong impressions? Do they present scriptural incidents as they really are?

   b. Do the pictures present typical and realistic situations rather than the exceptional and unrealistic?

3. Will the pictures encourage pupil participation? Stimulate conversation?

4. Are the pictures suited to particular age groups?

   a. Are the pictures related to the lives of the pupils?

   b. Are the pictures for younger children simple and well outlined? Do they contain little detail and avoid the symbolic?

   c. As pictures are considered for all age groups, is there a gradual increase in the amount of detail, leading to more complex pictures for older pupils?

5. Will the pictures gain interest?

   a. Do the pictures show action? Is something happening?

   b. Do the pictures portray familiar incidents and subjects?

   c. Do the pictures have artistic quality? Is there good organization? A center of interest?

   d. Do the pictures show natural color?

   e. Are the pictures clear and sharp?

   f. Are they large enough?

6. Do the pictures present a positive message?

PICTURES OF CHRIST

Some Christians question the advisability of using pictures of Jesus Christ. They feel that since there are no accurate pictorial records of His features, artists' conceptions should not be used. Others feel that the use of pictures of Christ may lead to a form of "picture worship" rather than to true worship of the living Christ.

These arguments are certainly worthy of consideration, and it is agreed that Christians must guard against "idolatry" in any form. However, since it is almost impossible to keep children from seeing some of the pictures of

Fig. 87. Pictures of Christ can be used effectively to demonstrate His reality to children (Regier)

Christ, "why not provide them with the best the ages have produced?"[2] The use of these pictures need not lead to "picture worship"; rather, with the proper explanation that pictures of Christ are merely artists' conceptions, they can aid true worship. They can help children, particularly, to visualize the fact that Jesus is a Person who was once a baby, who grew to be a boy and then a man (see Fig. 87).

Adults, of course, do not need pictures of Christ to aid their imagination. Nevertheless, Sallman's pictures of "Christ at the Door," or of "Christ the Pilot" provide inspiration for both young people and adults.

FILING PICTURES

In order to be usable as effective visual aids, flat pictures must be easily accessible to Christian workers. Very large pictures may be mounted on durable cardboard and filed edgewise in a cardboard box or in a wooden file made from plywood. Small pictures may be filed in 8½ x 11-inch manila folders and placed in a standard letter-size filing cabinet.

When first starting to organize a picture file in a regular letter-size filing cabinet, folders containing only the main titles should be used (see file outline that follows). As more and various types of pictures are collected, additional subfolders may be added. For example, all pictures of Christ may go into one folder tabbed "Pictures of Christ." When the collection becomes large enough to be subdivided, folders may be added, bearing such titles as "the Christmas Story," "Jesus as a Boy," and "Jesus Teaching."

Another approach in filing is to place all pictures of one kind in manila envelopes marked "the Christmas Story," "Jesus as a Boy," "Jesus Teaching," etc. These envelopes are then placed in one folder or section tabbed "Pictures of Christ."

The following outline is prepared for filing commercial prints:

Old Testament
    Creation
    Cain and Abel
    Abraham
    Isaac
    Jacob
    Joseph
    Moses
    Joshua
    Samuel
    Ruth
    Saul
    David
    Kings
    Daniel
    Other Prophets

New Testament
    John the Baptist
    Christ
        Birth
        Childhood
        The Temptation
        On the Hillside
        With the Children
        Teaching
        Miracles
        Parables
        With Friends and Disciples
        Passion Week
        Resurrection
        Post Resurrection
        Head of Christ
        Others (At the Door, As Pilot, etc.)

Apostles
    Peter
    John
    Stephen
    Paul
    Others

Modern Scenes
    Animals
    Going to Church
    Helping
    Missions
    Nature
    Praying
    Bible
    Sharing
    Singing
    Worship

The following outline is prepared for filing flat pictures that come from other sources; therefore, titles for filing religious prints are few.

Religious
    Christ
    New Testament
    Old Testament
    Worship
    Missions
Secular
    Agriculture
    Architecture
    Botany
        Flowers
        General
    Contrast
        Age-Youth
        Past-Present
    Events
        Personal
        Historical
    Food

Holidays
    Christmas
    Easter
    Patriotic
    Thanksgiving
    Valentine's Day
Hygiene
Music
People
    Couples
    Families
    Foreign
    Individuals
        Babies
        Children
        Adolescent
        Adult
        Aged
    Mixed groups
Scenery
    Fall
    Night
    Sky
    Spring
    Summer
    Winter
    Water
Sports
Travel
    Airplanes
    Automobile
    Boat and ship
    Bus and truck
    Trains

PRESERVING FLAT PICTURES

Both commercially made pictures and those from other sources should be mounted and given a protective covering to keep them from becoming damaged and soiled. Pupils as well as teachers handle these pictures, and any length of service is bound to bring wear and tear.

Mounts. Mounts should be of substantial material. Temporary mounting may be done on various colored pieces of construction paper; more permanent mounting should be done on poster board or cardboard which can be purchased inexpensively at art or school supply stores. Cardboard sheets often found in men's new shirts or when they are returned from the laundry, or cardboard cartons serve as excellent mounting materials.

Cloth backing will also serve as permanent mounts. Chartex is a cambric material coated on one side with a heat-seal adhesive and is used for mounting pictures, maps, charts, etc. Chartex is available in an assortment of cut sheets and roll sizes.

When a mount is used with borders that extend beyond the picture, the color should be chosen on the basis of the colors in the pictures. Ordinarily light mounts should be used with dark pictures and vice versa. The extending borders should be proportioned so that the bottom margin on each picture is the widest, the top margin slightly narrower, and the sides still narrower than the top. For effective filing, mounts should be as uniform in size as possible.

Submounts may also be used to add to the attractiveness of pictures. The margins of the submount on each picture should be even on all sides.

Adhesives. Various adhesives may be used to fasten pictures to mounts. Rubber cement is the most effective since it leaves no wrinkles, excessive amounts can be removed with the fingers without soiling pictures or mounts, and pictures can be easily removed from the mounts without damage to either picture or mount. Although the adhesion from rubber cement is not as sturdy as glue or paste, it is permanent enough for most uses. A more permanent mounting may be obtained by applying the rubber cement to both the picture and the mount and allowing each to set for a couple minutes before pressing them together.

Pastes, bought or made, may also be used for more permanent mounting, but they must be used with more caution so that excessive amounts will not soil pictures or mounts. The Library of Congress suggests this formula for a homemade paste:

> ½ cup all-purpose or bread flour
> ½ cup cold water
> 3 cups boiling water
> Few drops formaldehyde
> 1½ teaspoons glycerin

Stir the flour and cold water together until the mixture is completely smooth. Add a little of the boiling water to the paste, stir until smooth, then add the paste to the rest of the boiling water. Cook slowly, stirring constantly, until the mixture is thick and smooth. Add the formaldehyde to prevent spoiling and to discourage insects. Add glycerin to improve flexibility.

The mixture should be quite thick, but thin enough to drop from the brush. It may be thinned with water if necessary. It should be entirely free from lumps. Strain through cheesecloth if necessary.[3]

Transparent gummed tapes may be used for pictures mounted on paper or cardboard materials the same size as the pictures. The tape should be carefully placed on the pictures and then fastened to the mounts. A special edging machine which will do a neat and rapid job may be purchased for this purpose.[4]

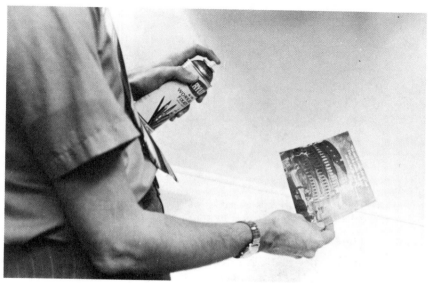

Fig. 88. Preserve pictures by spraying on a covering of clear plastic (Regier)

A protective covering. A spray of cellulose acetate or clear plastic may be used to cover pictures to protect them from dirt and wear (see Fig. 88). Coverings of cellophane or transparent plastic envelopes will also serve this purpose. A special transparent envelope can be easily made by cutting the front from a large manila envelope and covering the opening with cellophane. Pictures may be inserted and passed around the class for pupils to handle.

Another suggestion is the use of Saran Wrap which can be purchased at any grocery store. It is similar to cellophane, but it has a self-adhering quality. Saran Wrap should be cut so that there is a border about two inches wide on each edge of the picture; the picture is placed face downward on the Saran Wrap and the borders of the covering folded over the edges of the picture. The Saran Wrap will adhere without cement, paster or tape.

For a more permanent covering, use a laminating process. Lamination is achieved by means of heat and pressure in a special press (see Fig. 89).

Fig. 89. The laminating press is an ideal tool for laminating a protective sheet of plastic to a picture or a picture to a mount (Seal Inc.)

USING FLAT PICTURES

Flat pictures may be used with all age groups, but they have a more extensive use with children. They are excellent aids in telling Bible, missionary and character stories. They help to review, introduce new ideas, prepare settings, stimulate conversation, and to apply Christian truths to life experience. They aid in adding variety and in making meanings clear when teaching memory verses and new songs, and selected pictures may serve as meaningful interest centers in worship activities. They are primarily helpful in overcoming the barriers to communication.

Flat pictures may also be used with young people and adults. Sallman's "Christ at the Door," and da Vinci's "Last Supper," make excellent picture studies; they may be framed and placed in class or department rooms to add to the spiritual atmosphere. Other pictures may be used on posters or bulletin boards to impart certain truth or to promote special meetings and other activities. Young people and adults also enjoy the opportunity for service in collecting, mounting and filing pictures to be used by Christian workers in the various agencies of the church.

SPECIFIC PRINCIPLES FOR USE

1. Choose pictures to correlate with specific lessons and units of study.

2. Help pupils to read and understand pictures correctly by asking questions or by indicating important points for which to look.

3. Use a few pictures rather than many; don't confuse pupils by presenting too many ideas.

4. Motivate the pupils to ask questions and to make comments about the pictures. Ask them to look for and bring related pictures from home. Stimulate pupils to draw their own pictures.

5. Make sure all can see the details of pictures. With large groups, large pictures should be used unless small prints are projected on the screen with an opaque projector, or passed around the class.

6. Let small children touch as well as see pictures.

7. Use unique ways of displaying pictures at eye level; place them on a simple stand on a table or tack them on a bulletin board. Choose two or three outstanding pictures to frame and place on classroom or department room walls.

PHOTOGRAPHS

Interesting and useful black and white pictures or candid "snapshots" can be taken by both teachers and pupils. The majority of people today have at their disposal simple inexpensive cameras which can be used in a variety of ways in Christian education.

Sunday school teachers or other Christian workers can make helpful looseleaf notebooks in which they include a page for each pupil with whom they work. On this page can be placed a photograph of the pupil which has been taken by the teacher or secured from the pupil along with other vital information. This illustrated notebook will serve as a constant prayer reminder and as an effective record book (see Fig. 90).

Photographs may be taken of various activities of the church as are found in the vacation Bible school, the Sunday school, at camp, retreats, picnics, parties, etc. These pictures may be filed or placed in an album for pictorial records, or they may be used for publicity purposes. For example, photographs taken of vacation Bible school activities may be arranged neatly and interestingly on a bulletin board or poster before the current school starts.

Pupils should be encouraged to take their own photographs. A worthwhile project for each pupil or for an entire group which will correlate well with the creation story is to make a picture album illustrating "God's World" (see Fig. 91). Another valuable project would be a picture album entitled "My Church." Pictures of all the various activities in which pupils participate, as well as photos of the pastor and his wife and of other church leaders and classmates could be included. Difficult shots, such as the Sunday school class in action, could be taken by the department superintendent or some other supervisor. If each pupil is making his own album, the teacher can have reproductions made for each member of the class.

Observation trips provide exceptional opportunities for taking pictures if pupils are encouraged to bring their cameras. The teacher or leader can give guidance so that worthwhile photographs are taken. In class meetings following the observation trip, the group can select the choice pictures from all those taken and make a poster, a bulletin board display, or a picture scrapbook. Appropriate titles or captions should be included in order to identify the pictures and to show their relationship to the unit under study.

The Polaroid camera, which provides opportunity to make instant, on-the-spot photographs, can be used in a variety of ways to achieve significant objectives in Christian education (see Figs. 92-93).

POSTERS

Most Christian workers are familiar, to some extent at least, with posters.[5] Their value has been manifested by their extensive use in the secular world, where it is impossible to live without being greatly affected by their messages as they advertise merchandise, promote ideas, and announce coming events.

Two types of posters can be used in Christian education: posters made commercially and homemade posters.

POSTERS MADE COMMERCIALLY

Commercially made posters can be purchased from various publishing houses. Those with appropriate Scripture texts and illustrative pictures are valuable for use in the church and equally effective when posted in places of business or other places that permit them. Publishing houses that prepare curriculum materials for use in the Sunday school and the vacation Bible school are usually ready to supply advertising posters at minimum rates; some religious organizations provide free posters to promote their materials (see Fig. 94).

HOMEMADE POSTERS

Homemade posters have advantages over commercially made posters because they can be prepared for every occasion, they reflect a personal touch, they are less expensive, and they provide valuable creative experiences for those who plan and make them. Artistic talent in the church among young and old should be discovered and put to use. Young people particularly who

Fig. 90. Using an inexpensive camera for taking candid pictures of Sunday school pupils to prepare picture notebooks, bulletin board displays, etc. (*Teach*)

Fig. 91. A student taking pictures to prepare a picture album illustrating the creation story (*Teach*)

Fig. 92. Taking a Polaroid picture (Polaroid)

Fig. 93. After a few seconds the photographer has a finished Polaroid print (Polaroid)

Fig. 94. A bulletin board display of commercially made posters which can be
used for a variety of purposes (Regier)

are studying art in high school should be elected to serve on publicity committees or given special assignments in poster-making.

Poster-making can also become a group project. Ideas discussed by the group can be further developed, painted or sketched by artistic-minded participants.

USING HOMEMADE POSTERS

Homemade posters have many uses as they serve as visual reminders for regular and special meetings of the church. Unique posters should be used periodically to promote youth meetings and church social activities, while simple posters may be used again and again to remind people of monthly Sunday school teachers' and officers' conferences, and of board or regular committee meetings. Posters changed periodically may be used weekly to remind people of the various prayer services and missionary meetings of the church. Caution must be taken, however, that the use of this effective medium of communication is not overdone and that the use of new ideas will add variety and interest. As with anything else that becomes commonplace, people soon fail to see what is actually there.

Poster contests among junior and junior high youngsters are enjoyed by those who participate, and they provide valuable experiences in creativity. All posters that are made should be recognized, but the best ones should be selected and used in the church and placed in store windows to advertise the annual vacation Bible school or camp program.

Young people will consider it an opportunity for service to be able to make posters to promote special evangelistic meetings as well as Bible, missionary, and Sunday school conferences. Remember, however, that all posters placed in store windows and other places of business should be displayed only after permission is granted from the owners, and out-of-date posters should always be promptly removed.

Posters made by teachers and pupils may also be used as valuable teaching aids. Unique outlines and charts prepared on poster board may be used to focus attention and to add variety to teaching methods. Various sized letters, attractive colors, drawings and sketches, and pictures with captions provide many possibilities for preparing outstanding teaching posters to be tacked on bulletin boards, fastened to classroom walls, placed on easels, or held by instructors or pupils (see Fig. 95).

WELL-MADE POSTERS

Posters, like flat pictures, should contain a center of interest. One outstanding idea should be easily seen and understood, so elaborate and irrelevant detail should be avoided. Subordinate ideas should be built around

Fig. 95. Using a homemade poster as a teaching aid (*Teach*)

the central truth, with key words and phrases standing out prominently. Every poster should be neat, well proportioned, and attractive.

TECHNIQUES AND MATERIALS

Good poster-making need not be left only to the artistic, for special devices may be used to do a satisfactory job. Techniques used for drawings and sketches may be applied to making posters, with the opaque projector and the pantograph serving very well. Proportional squares may also be used. A good picture file and an album of photographs provide many pictures that can be used on posters, and a stencil alphabet will aid in preparing neat legends.

Simple posters may be made with a ruler, a box of crayons, and a piece of poster board. However, to prepare all types of posters so as to add variety and to gain interest, the following additional materials should be available: colored pencils, poster paints, india ink, a ruling pen, a T-square, brushes for lettering and painting, and colored construction paper.

MURALS

Murals serve as special projects for all ages.[6] For example, a group of children under guidance may prepare a mural to illustrate the six days of creation to correlate with their study of the creation story. It might consist of a series of pictures, either drawn, cut out of construction paper, or taken from a well-developed picture file. Other murals might be large single

Fig. 96. A window mural (Campbell)

scenes depicting various aspects of worship or the Christian life. These murals can be displayed on chalkboards, bulletin boards, or on rolls of paper fastened to walls. During special seasons of the year, children also enjoy preparing window murals which may be painted on the glass or prepared with silhouettes and colored lights (see Fig. 96).

Older groups will enjoy making murals displaying missionary effort in certain areas, the historical development of Christianity, or various Bible scenes. Drawings, lettering, photography and many devices may be used to prepare these unique projects. They will serve not only as valuable creative experiences for groups who make them, but they will also serve as valuable teaching aids for others who see them.

Discussion Questions

1. What steps can be taken to start a picture file in the average church?
2. In addition to those suggested in this chapter, what ways can be used to involve pupils in the learning process when drawings are used? Flat pictures? Photographs? Posters? Murals?

Special Projects

1. Practice drawing the simple figures and sketches which are illustrated on page 115. Also create new ones. Be prepared to demonstrate these quickly and with ease before the group. Use the chalkboard, a piece of drawing paper, newsprint or some other suitable material.

2. Prepare a drawing by means of the opaque projector. Demonstrate the rapidity and simplicity of this technique. (This process can actually be done before the group or be prepared as an individual assignment.)

3. Prepare a set of folders for filing flat pictures clipped from magazines, books, pamphlets, newspapers, calendars and other sources. When starting, use just the main topics listed on pp. 124-25. Subfolders can be added later as the need arises.

4. Bring to class several well-mounted pictures which have been clipped from magazines and other sources. Show how correct colors for mountings can be chosen by experimentation.

5. Make a scrapbook of photographs and legends which could be prepared by a group of boys and girls. Show what could motivate this project and how it can be used in the church.

6. Prepare a series of teaching posters (this could be a class project). Illustrate how these can be used. Also prepare several posters which could be used to advertise the Sunday school, the vacation Bible school, the youth meeting, etc.

7. Make a mural that could be prepared by a group of boys and girls, and one that a group of young people could make. What could motivate these projects? Discuss their value.

9

Overhead Transparencies

When this book on audiovisuals was first published in 1958, I included two paragraphs about the overhead projector. In fact, I stated the following in dead earnestness: "Although this type of projector has many advantages, it is not advisable to consider purchasing this machine for use in the church until some of the other, more versatile projectors are purchased and utilized."

Today, of course, this statement is almost unbelievable, in fact, very amusing. But it illustrates what has taken place in the last several years. I would now put the overhead projector at the top of the list and classify it as the most versatile of all teaching tools. This is why I'm devoting a whole chapter to this one tool. Technologically, it has been improved temendously, the price is reasonable, and a multitude of materials can be prepared easily and inexpensively.

Regarding these developments, Richard Smith notes:

> The overhead projector is certainly no newcomer to the field of instructional devices. However, its size and expense kept it out of reach of most educators. . . . With the advent of the low-cost, lightweight projectors of the past five years, the overhead has suddenly become the darling of instructional devices—perhaps rightly so, as it has an extremely unique contribution to make in the realm of instructional media.[1]

The Projector

The overhead projector is used at the front of the classroom as you face your students. The material can be projected in a completely lighted room, although the image on the screen can be sharpened by turning out several lights at the front of the room. This, however, is not necessary as you will obtain an excellent image even when all of the lights are left on.

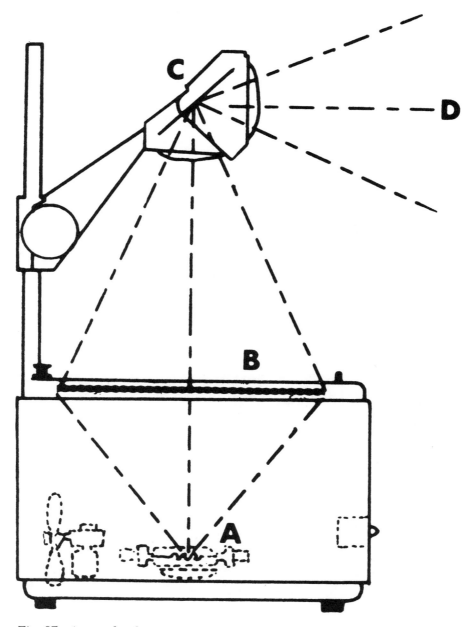

Fig. 97. An overhead projector can provide brilliant images since the optical system employs a light beam which shines directly through the transparency. (A) light source (B) stage where transparency is placed (C) projector head and (D) light beam to the screen (Charles Beseler Co.)

Fig. 98. Projection Optics Co. Inc.

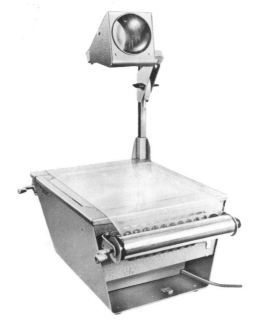

Fig. 99. Buhl Optical Co.

Fig. 100. Bell and Howell

Fig. 101. H. Wilson

Some of the advantages of this teaching tool are obvious. You can face your students, maintain eye contact, point out material you want to emphasize, and as is shown later, you can utilize various techniques to control what you want your audience to see.

As can be seen in Figure 97, the overhead projector has a horizontal stage, which means you can write on the surface and use the projector in the same way you would use a chalkboard. This, however, is not its greatest asset. As is demonstrated in a later section, its greatest advantage is in the variety of transparencies which can be prepared and projected.

A number of excellent projectors are available from various companies. (see Figs. 98-101).[2] The recommended type is the one which has its light source beneath the platen or stage, as illustrated in Figure 97.

Here are some specific suggestions for operating the overhead projector:

1. Project at an angle in the room. This way students won't have to look continually at the light reflection on the screen when it is left on for long periods of time. Also, this enables everyone to see even though the instructor is standing in front of the class.

2. Keep the screen as high from the floor as possible. This will also assist students in seeing the projected image.

3. Eliminate keystoning by tilting the screen, with the top edge of the screen farthest from the wall (see Figs. 102-3).

4. Focus the projector by turning the knob which raises or lowers the lens head. Once this is set you can rest assured that your projected image is in clear focus.

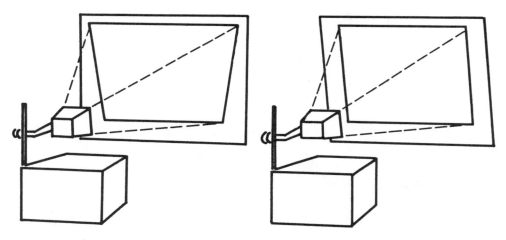

Fig. 102. Improper angle resulting in keystoning (Regier)   Fig. 103. Proper angle which has eliminated keystoning (Regier)

TRANSPARENCIES

"In the early 1960's, a standard college audiovisual textbook observed that there were very few commercially produced educational transparencies available. Just a few years later thousands were on the market."[3]

Though religious sources do not have as many transparencies to offer as secular sources, the years ahead will see an increasing supply of commercially produced transparencies on biblical and biblically related themes. But, as with many visuals, perhaps the best materials will always be those which are tailor-made by individual teachers to meet their own particular needs. Several types of transparencies can be prepared for this purpose.[4] (See Appendix II for places where materials for making the following transparencies can be obtained.)

HANDMADE TRANSPARENCIES

Handmade transparencies can be easily made by writing or drawing on clear acetate or reprocessed X-ray film. A regular grease pencil works well in creating black lines on the screen. Material can be prepared in color, however, by using special grease pencils and plastic fiber-tip pens which are available from a number of distributors. Colored adhesive film is also available for making simple handmade transparencies. When the backing is removed from the film, it can be placed in position on the acetate base, thus giving a beautiful colored image. Packages containing this film usually include instructions for completing this process (see Fig. 104).

Fig. 104. Teachers' do-it-yourself transparency kit (Highland Systems)

Another approach to homemade visuals for use on the overhead projector is to use an acetate roll. Most projectors can be equipped with such a roll which makes it possible to crank visuals across the stage of the projector. This way you can prepare the material before class and then reveal the visuals as you need them during the class session.

There are several disadvantages with this approach. For example, visuals are of necessity forced into a sequence, and if you wish to refer back to a previous visual you will need to turn the roll back to that spot. With separate frames, this, of course, is not necessary.

HEAT-TRANSFER TRANSPARENCIES

This type of transparency, often called a thermal transparency, can be prepared on any standard infrared office copy machine. Transparencies can be made in a matter of seconds by copying from newspapers, magazines and books. Line drawings made with a pencil or india ink, or typewritten material prepared with a carbon ribbon also make clear transparencies. Both positive and negative heat-transfer film is available in various colors.

The original material to be copied can be on fully opaque or translucent paper. The artwork, however, should be as opaque as possible in order to produce a sharp transparency.

Generally, thermal machines operate in the same way:

1. Place the master faceup on a flat surface.

2. Place the film on the master with the coated side against the master (notice notch in the film which indicates the coated side).

3. Adjust the heat control on the thermal copier. (Tip: To avoid wasting film, cut a regular piece of film into a number of narrow strips. Use these strips to test the exposure setting of the machine.)

4. Feed the film and master into the machine.

DIAZO TRANSPARENCIES

A more professional-looking and colorful transparency can be made by using the diazo process. Though it is a more complex process, it is still a relatively simple one.

The following steps are suggested in making a diazo transparency:

1. Prepare a master on a sheet of translucent paper. Especially prepared translucent diazo paper or drafting vellum is best.

2. Artwork should be done with india ink. For special effects use press-on letters, stencil lettering, guides, etc. (Note: All opaque areas on the master will produce colored areas on the film.)

For large areas, ink both sides of the master so that it is completely opaque. To short-cut this process, use opaque paper. Cut out the shape you want and tape it to your master. (Note: Use only Scotch Magic Transparent tape). Any mistake in your artwork can be cut out with a razor.

3. Remove a sheet of diazo film. Dark colors work best for lettering; pastels are not too readable. (Reseal the package so that the film is not unnecessarily exposed to room light).

4. Prepare a sandwich with the following materials:

a. Place the diazo film, coated side up, on a flat surface. (Note: The coated side can be detected by referring to the manufacturer's instruction sheet, or by touching the tip of your tongue to the film. The sensitized side will give a slight taste of salt.

b. Place the master facedown on the film.

5. If using a commercial diazo printer, place the sandwich in the printer tray, and place the glass covering over the sandwich.

6. Insert the tray into the diazo printer, and expose the film. Follow the exposure instructions which are printed by the manufacturer.

7. Remove the tray from the printer, take film from the sandwich, and place it in a jar, containing 26-28 percent Baume ammonia fumes.

8. Remove transparency from jar when fully developed. (Note: Ammonia fumes are strong and should not be inhaled).

9. For more permanent and effective use, mount your transparencies.

MAKING YOUR OWN DIAZO PRINTER

Unfortunately, commercially made diazo printers are rather expensive, but an inexpensive printer can be made to do an effective job.

The following plans for the diazo printer first appeared in 1962 in the magazine *Audiovisual Instruction*. Since then it has been released in a separate tear sheet developed by Dr. Joel A. Benedict, Audio-Visual Center, Arizona State University.

This diazo printer really works. A number of my students at Dallas Theological Seminary have used them to make very professional-looking transparencies. In fact, when it is done correctly, you cannot distinguish a transparency made with this homemade printer from one which has been made with a commercial unit.

To make it more convenient for you to build this kit, Arizona State University has assembled all of the necessary parts into a kit. These parts include the following:

1 Plexiglas tube 3-inch diameter, 13 inches long
1 fluorescent ballast
1 fluorescent starter
1 socket for starter
2 fluorescent lamp holders

1 G.E. F 15 T 8-B1
fluorescent 15-watt black light
1 electric cord and plug
1 wire nut
1 piece of 12 × 12-inch canvas taped to plexiglas tube

All these parts are packed in a special box and may be had for only $15. Send your order to Audio-Visual Center, Arizona State University, Tempe, Arizona.

The only other parts needed are those for the plywood box, which may be built in any school shop according to the following plans:

PARTS SCHEDULE

A 2 sides, 5⅜ × 18¾ inches
B 1 top, 5¾ × 18 inches
C 1 bottom, 5¾ × 18 inches
D 2 ends, 5⅜ × 5¾ inches
E 2 Plexiglas tube supports, 4 × 5¾ inches

ASSEMBLY INSTRUCTIONS

The parts for the box may be cut from a piece of plywood 36 inches wide and 18¾ inches long and ⅜ inches thick. The box is completely assembled with glue and wire brads and then cut open as shown in Figure 105, making two equal halves. The length of the box may vary slightly, depending on the type of fluorescent sockets used.

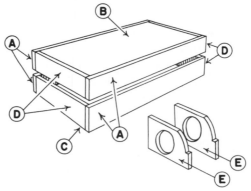

Fig. 105. Assembling the box
for a homemade printer

The round hole in part E is the same as the outside diameter of the Plexiglas tube. The center of the hole is 1¾ inches from the bottom of the support. The tube must rotate freely when mounted. The hole may be cut slightly larger than the tube and lined with a strip of felt if desired. Be certain that the fluorescent lamp is in the center of the Plexiglas tube when mounted. A small block of wood may be placed at each end in the bottom of the box to prevent the Plexiglas tube from slipping endwise (See Fig. 106).

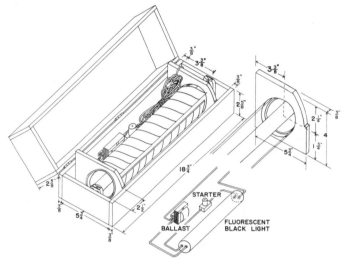

Fig. 106. Assembling the homemade printer

Following are illustrated instructions for making transparencies with this homemade printer (see Figs. 107-116).

OVERLAY TRANSPARENCIES

One of the most valuable techniques that can be used with the overhead projector is to make use of overlay transparencies (see Fig. 117). With this type of visual you are building up a concept or an idea step by step. From the standpoint of effective communication, there are several advantages in using an overlay:

1. By showing only one part at a time you do not confuse the viewer by bombarding him with the total idea.

2. By revealing one idea at a time, you can maintain control of the class. All minds can be focused on one idea—the one you're talking about—rather than a variety of ideas that might be vying for a student's attention.

Fig. 107. Basic equipment and materials for making a Diazo transparency with a homemade printer.

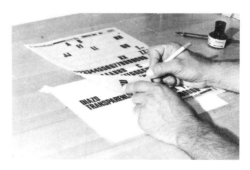

Fig. 108. Preparing a transparency. Place choice of opaque material on translucent master. For example, this figure illustrates the use of press-on letters. India ink, opaque cutouts, and tapes may also be used.

Fig. 109. Making an overlay. Prepare a second master. Note: As illustrated in this figure, line up the corners properly to assure proper registration.

Fig. 110. Preparing sandwich of materials. Place in this order: (1) backing sheet, (2) unexposed film, (3) prepared master.

Fig. 111. Rolling sandwich around the tube. Allow a light to pass through the master to the film.

Fig. 112. Making final preparations. Pull the vinyl cover tight around the tube and close the printer lid before turning on the light.

Fig. 113. Exposing film. Leave in box for proper period of time (You will need to experiment with exposure time); remove the exposed film from the printer and place in the ammonia jar. Note: Don't inhale ammonia fumes.

Fig. 114. Exposing the transparency in the ammonia jar. Expose until it reaches the intensity you desire. Note: You can see the process taking place as illustrated in this figure.

Fig. 115. Mounting the transparency. In this case, since there are two base transparencies (called statics) and one overlay, mount the statics on the back of the mount and mount the overlay on the front. Use tape to hinge the overlay.

Fig. 116. Projecting the completed transparency (Figs. 106-15 photographed by Regier and Focht)

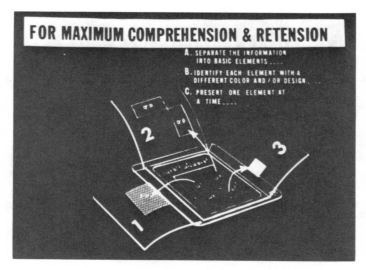

Fig. 117. The flip-over system may be used to present information sequencially. The number of overlay which can be used is theoretically unlimited as long as they are attached in the proper sequence. Practically, however, reduction and light output in mechanical considerations limits the number of overlays as to maximum of five or six (Technifax Corp.)

3. "Partial revelation" also creates an attitude of expectancy. In other words, "What's coming next?"

4. Also, many ideas are complex and they can only be understood adequately as the idea is built up and explained one concept at a time (see Figs. 118-22).

Mounting Transparencies

Richard Smith has suggested the following steps for mounting transparencies.[5]

STEPS IN MOUNTING A STATIC TRANSPARENCY

1. Work on a clean, bright surface. Dust and dirt can easily scratch and permanently damage the transparency film. A bright or light-colored surface will make the visual show up better and enable you to properly center the transparency on the frame.

2. Keep the base line of the visual parallel to the edge of the mount. Tilted visuals look awkward when projected.

3. Tack the film to the mount at two film corners.

4. Check to see that it is properly centered. Unless it is a temporary transparency, tape down the film on all four sides, using a nonoozing tape that will resist drying out, such as Scotch No. 810.

Fig. 118. Starting with the base transparency

Fig. 119. Adding overlay No. 1

Fig. 120. Adding overlay No. 2

Fig. 121. Adding overlay No. 3

Fig. 122. Adding overlay No. 4 (Regier)

STEPS IN MOUNTING DYNAMIC OVERLAYS

1. Place all overlays on the static (that is, the base transparency) and check registration. (If they have been exposed in a uniform manner, you can mount all overlays with the emulsion side down. They will lie better this way as the film curl will be uniform.)

2. Check for adequate marginal area on overlays for hinging. (You may need to move the static to accommodate the overlays.)

3. Mount static, taping all four sides.

4. Add overlays in same sequence in which they will be used, hinging each one carefully to keep it in register. Special adhesive hinges are sold for this purpose and are well worth having. If the overlay sequence is absolutely rigid, you can hinge all from the same side. If a flexible sequence is desired, hinge overlays from different sides of the mount.

TRANSPARENCY EXAMPLE

A variety of graphic materials can be used to communicate Christian truth by means of overhead transparencies: charts, graphs, diagrams, illustrations, maps, etc. In some instances you can very effectively use printed material only. Following are some examples of biblical and biblically related visuals (see Figs. 123-36).

UTILIZING OVERHEAD TRANSPARENCIES

Duane Litfin has outlined the following suggestions for effectively using the overhead projector:[6]

1. Be sure the overhead is focused properly. Too often an entire presentation is given with the image focused improperly on the screen, which makes for difficult viewing on the part of the audience.

2. Do not keep looking back at the screen. If the overhead has been properly focused in the beginning, the material will appear on the screen exactly as it does on the projector stage. Thus, full advantage may be taken of the benefit of continuous eye contact with the audience.

3. Do all pointing on the projector stage. A pointer, pencil, or even a finger used on the projector stage is much more effective visually than an attempt to point out something on the screen itself. This also eliminates the rather distracting occurrence of having the user being projected upon as he tries to point out something on the screen. "If your hand tends to shake while holding the pointing device, touch it to the transparency to steady it."[7] Generally, the only exception to this rule occurs when a negative slide is being projected. In this case, pointing must be done on the screen.

4. Do not lay hands or fingers on the stage except when pointing. This causes distractive movements on the screen.[8]

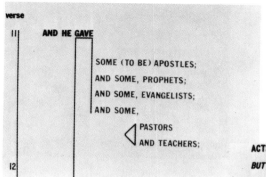

Fig. 123. Ephesians 4:11

(Figs. 123-36, Audiovisual Center,
Dallas Theological Seminary)

Fig. 124. Acts 1:8

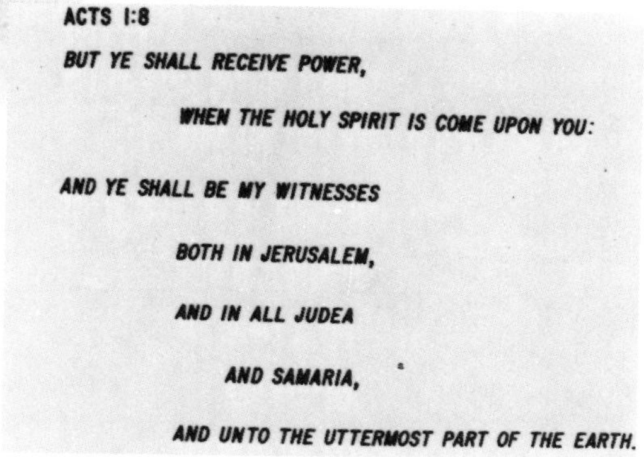

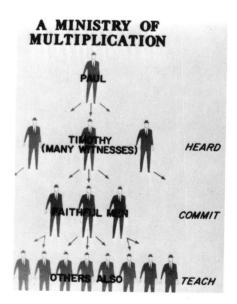

Fig. 125. 2 Timothy 2:2

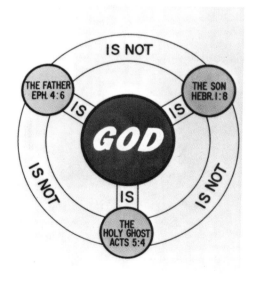

Fig. 126. The Trinity

Fig. 127. Man's relation to God's plan

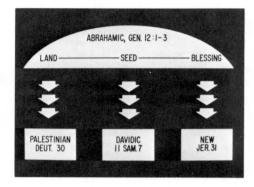

Fig. 128. The Abrahamic covenant

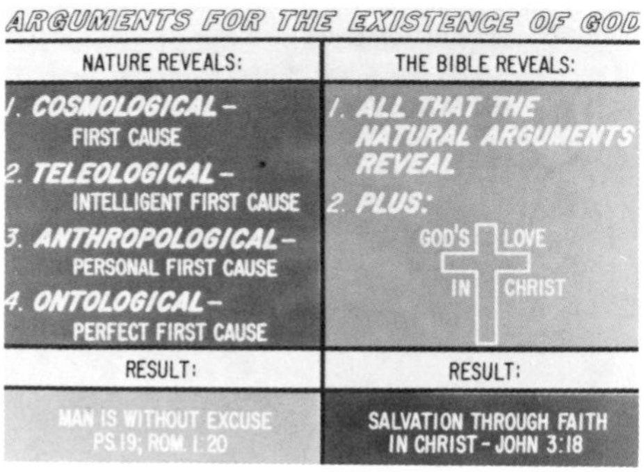

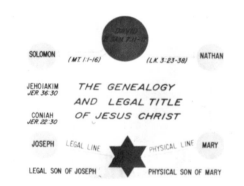

Fig. 129. Arguments for the existence
of God

Fig. 130. The genealogy and legal title
of Jesus Christ

Fig. 131. Israel's trip from Egypt to
Canaan

Fig. 132. The laver

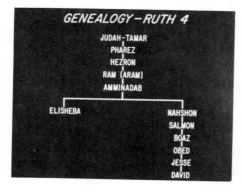

Fig. 133. Genealogies—Ruth 4

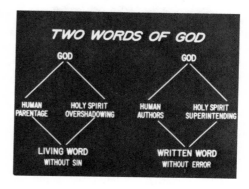

Fig. 134. Two words of God

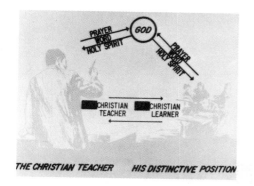

Fig. 135. The Christian teacher—his
distinctive position

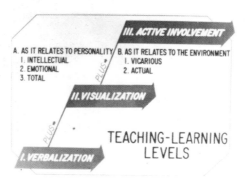

Fig. 136. Teaching learning levels

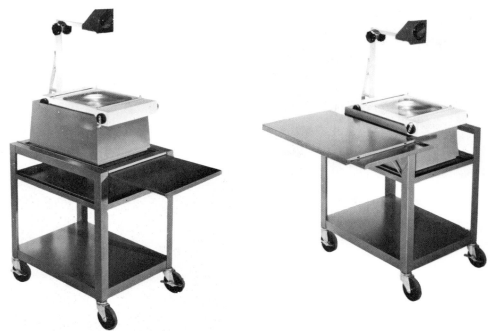

Fig. 137. Hi-low table—stand up, sit down positions shown (Wilson Co.)

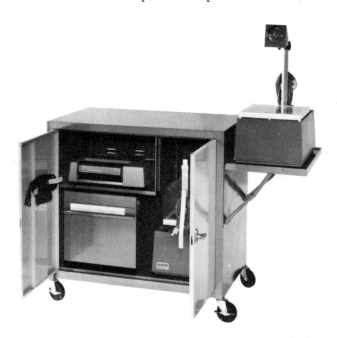

Fig. 138. Mobile overhead center (Wilson Co.)

5. Have the transparencies arranged in order so that all unnecessary shuffling of materials is eliminated.[9]

6. Place the transparencies on the stage before turning on the lamp.[10] This is much more effective visually than trying to place the transparency on the platen with the screen already illuminated.

7. Keep the transparency even on the projector stage. Do not allow the light to project around its outside edges. This allows the slides to project evenly on the screen and centers the light for the best visual effect.

8. Use the lighted screen to the best advantage. Shultz explains:

> The teacher is able to maintain complete classroom control and interest in a lesson by simply turning a switch on and off. When you wish to direct student attention to you, you turn the projector off. When you wish to direct attention back to the visual material, you turn the projector on.[11]

9. Hold the transparency mount when flipping overlays. The flipping can cause the transparency to move distractingly on the stage.[12]

10. Do not walk from side to side in front of the projector in such a way as to cast a shadow on the screen. This is most distracting to the viewers.

11. Try to keep the information towards the top of the stage.[13] This places it at the top of the screen for peak visibility. In presentations where the progress of information moves from the top to bottom, the projector head may be tilted so that the material previously at the bottom of the screen is projected near the top, while the material previously at the top has moved off the screen altogether. [See Figs. 137-38.]

10

Motion Pictures

ONE WEDNESDAY MORNING, Bill Halley, president of the senior young people's group at Grace Church, was deep in thought as he sat in a large easy chair in the living room of his home. *What can I do?* he thought. *Lately our youth meetings have been so dull and uninteresting.*

As Bill turned the situation over in his mind, suddenly he was struck with an idea. He hurriedly left the chair in which he was sitting and crossed the room to the telephone. After checking in the phone book, he dialed a number. In a few seconds a voice at the other end of the line answered, "Religious Film Center—Miss McCarthy speaking."

"This is Bill Halley from Grace Church. Do you have any good films that would appeal to young people?"

"Yes, we do," answered Miss McCarthy.

"I'd like to show one this coming Sunday evening. Would you have any suggestions?"

"This *coming* Sunday evening?" repeated the secretary in a surprised manner. "I'm sorry. All of the outstanding films are usually booked weeks in advance."

"Oh!" answered Bill in a rather dejected tone.

"Just a moment," replied Miss McCarthy after a moment's hesitation.

In a short time she returned. "Hello, Mr. Halley. In checking our list again, I find we have two films that haven't been booked for this weekend. They *may* serve your purpose."

After hearing the titles of the two films, Bill selected the one that sounded fairly appropriate for the youth meeting. He concluded the telephone con-

157

versation by asking that the film be sent immediately; he was definitely planning to use it Sunday evening.

Bill arrived at the church in what he thought was "plenty of time." A few young people had already gathered. As he walked in with the projector, screen and the film, he could hear various comments such as, "Oh, good, we're going to have a movie tonight," and "Wonderful! I didn't have my part prepared for the 'supposed-to-be' meeting anyway."

Bill immediately began to set up the equipment, but he soon discovered a few problems. He didn't have an extension cord that was the proper length, and it was too early in the evening to be dark enough to show the film without covering the windows with something. Bill gave some quick orders and asked several young people to look for curtains. As he was wondering how to get an extension cord, John Harper, the vice-president, came in the door.

"John," called Bill. "Would you get the meeting started? Lead in some lively choruses and testimonies or something!"

John, a bit surprised, nodded approvingly.

Bill rushed off to find another extension cord. When he returned several minutes later, it was already past time for the meeting to start. He motioned to John, who was busily looking through a chorus book, and again reminded him to get the meeting started. John, rather hesitantly, stood to his feet, called to the pianist and asked her to come and play.

The meeting was soon in progress, while Bill continued to set up the equipment. Since he had not used this particular projector before, he had some trouble threading it; but as he referred to the threading chart that came with the machine, he finally succeeded in getting everything ready. John was still trying to fill time and keep things moving as he asked for favorite choruses and testimonies. When he received a signal from Bill that the film was ready to be shown, he sat down and Bill came to the front of the room.

"We've had a few problems, but we're ready to get started. I know you're going to like the film. The name of it is ——," and at this point Bill had to inform the group that in the rush he had forgotten the title. But he assured the young people that it was "good."

After the lights were turned out, the film showing started. But no sooner was the projector turned on than it was evident by a distinct noise that something was wrong with the machine. After turning the projector off and asking for the room lights, Bill discovered that he had forgotten to form one of the "loops." With this corrected and a sigh of relief, the film showing was again in progress.

It wasn't long until Bill discovered that the film was more appropriate for older children than for young people, but it *was* interesting, for which Bill was supremely happy.

Fortunately, all went well until near the end of the film. When Bill looked at his watch, it was already a few minutes past the regular dismissal time. The evening church service was to start in a few minutes. He hadn't realized that the time had passed so quickly while he was preparing to show the film. Then, too, the film was a little longer than he had expected. There were still five minutes of film on the reel. By the time it was finally over, church had already started. The pastor, a bit disturbed, had looked in to see what was causing the delay, but had quickly disappeared into the sanctuary.

As soon as the motion picture was over and the lights were turned on, most of the young people began to leave.

"Wait a minute," called Bill. The young people—some halfway up the stairs, some standing, and some still seated—turned to see what their president wanted.

"I know you're in a hurry," continued Bill, "but there's the problem of financing this film. I guess the only way to defray the expense is to take an offering."

"How much is the rental?" asked one of the fellows who was already halfway out the door.

"Twelve dollars," replied Bill rather hesitantly.

"Wow!" said one of the girls. Some of the young people looked surprised and others frowned.

"That's going to cost each one of us quite a bit," said John, the vice-president. "I didn't bring enough money with me for an extra offering."

"I guess it's my fault you didn't know about the expense," said Bill rather apologetically. "I shouldn't have been in such a hurry in renting the film. I guess we'd better wait until next week for the offering. I'll take care of the bill for now."

As soon as all of the young people had left for the sanctuary, Bill slowly, and with a somewhat bewildered expression, began to put away the equipment. Even though there was time, he did not go to the service that night. He was too discouraged. He just went home.

General Principles

Fortunately, not every film showing is like the one just illustrated. However, a number of similar situations are taking place in many, many churches due to the fact that pastors, teachers, and other Christian workers are not taking into consideration the basic principles for using projected aids.

CAREFUL SELECTION

Projected aids should be selected with utmost caution since all those available are not appropriate or worthwhile. Only the specific aids that best fit and meet the needs of the local situation should be rented or purchased. If at all possible they should fit into the planned curriculum; they should be used with units of study, for special meetings, and for special days.

SELF-PREPARATION

A person who uses projected aids must be thoroughly prepared by previewing the materials and then carefully planning the session. This involves observing, praying, discovering the most effective use, thinking through the time schedule, and preparing an approach and an application.

ROOM PREPARATION

To be used effectively, projected aids must be shown in a well-prepared room. There must be adequate facilities for darkening the room, proper ventilation, and a satisfactory seating arrangement. All equipment should be set up and made ready for use before the viewers arrive. (For proper room arrangement, see Figs. 139-40).

GROUP PREPARATION

When preparing a group to see a film, filmstrips, or set of slides, the plans made during the period of "self-preparation" should be carried out. There may be a correlated Scripture reading and a time for singing especially selected songs. Certain questions which are related to the content of the projected pictures may be given to the group, or certain points to look for may be enumerated by the leader.

FOLLOW-UP

Follow-up should lead to life application, which makes this final point exceedingly important. Without it much of the value gained through careful selection and preparation will be lost. Follow-up might consist of a thought-provoking discussion; several minutes might be given so that the questions given before the showing might be answered individually and then discussed together. If appropriate, an invitation for salvation or dedication of life may be extended; there may be a special season for prayer, a challenging message, or the group could be led to launch a special project or do additional research on a related subject.

ANALYSIS OF BILL'S PROBLEMS

In evaluating the young people's meeting described at the beginning of

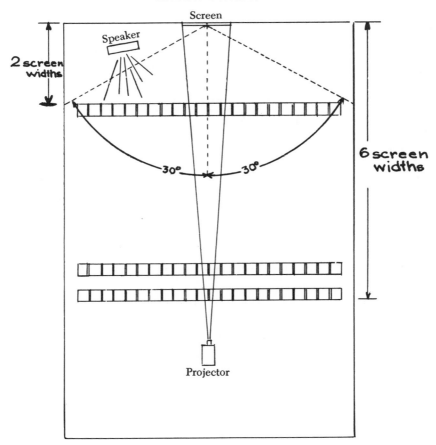

Fig. 139. Proper room arrangement (top view)

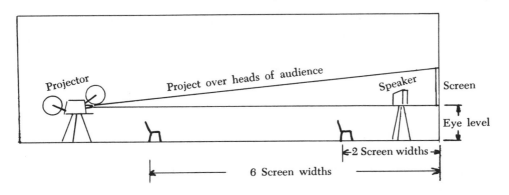

Fig. 140. Proper room arrangement (side view)

this chapter, it is clearly evident that Bill failed to apply each one of the general principles for using projected aids.

First of all, his action in renting the film was a "spur of the moment" decision. This was improper for several reasons:

1. There was no time to discover what would be an appropriate and worthwhile film; it was not reserved in advance.

2. There was no opportunity to discuss the choice of financial problem with the group; no one was informed, including the pastor.

3. The film was not chosen on the basis of need, nor was it worked into a curriculum unit or a series of meetings.

Second, the problems faced on the evening the film was shown gave evidence that there was no preplanning.

1. The film had not been previewed by Bill or any of the group members.

2. The preservice had not been planned with correlated songs, Scripture reading, prayer, or other preparatory activities.

3. The room had not been prepared; provision was not made for darkening the windows.

4. The equipment had not been set up and checked.

5. The time element had not been carefully thought through, thus not leaving time for follow-up and application.

The results of this evening meeting may be classified as follows and applied to all such film showings:

1. The group missed much that could have been gained had they been prepared to receive the message of the film and then led to apply it to their lives.

2. The group was dissatisfied for several reasons: there was much confusion, the film was not geared to meet their particular needs, and there was the unsuspected financial burden.

3. Bill was unnecessarily burdened with all of the responsibilities of renting the film and showing it. This, in addition to poor preparation, resulted in discouragement.

4. The young people were late for the evening service, and Bill didn't attend.

Specific Principles for Selection and Use

A GROUP PROJECT

Time, effort and money are wasted when motion pictures are rented by one teacher or leader. They should be used so that as many people as possible can benefit from the showings. Usually, motion-picture films should be used in departmental or combined class meetings rather than in small groups or classes.

Due to the limited number of outstanding 16 mm. motion pictures, it is not always possible to select one that will fit into a unit of study; however, the film should always be chosen on the basis of needs.

The following example illustrates correct selection of a series of 16 mm. motion-picture films: A youth group in one church decided to conduct a series of meetings on the subject of "worship." The plan for six months of meetings was well outlined in advance and prepared to include subjects such as the importance of the Bible, prayer, music and stewardship in worship. The first main topic, the "Importance of the Bible in Worship," was divided into several subtopics, one being "How We Got Our English Bible." While a special committee was planning these meetings, the leader suggested that several appropriate films be used to show how the Bible came into being. Upon investigation, the group discovered that three excellent films were available on this subject. The dates were set, and films were ordered well in advance.

NOT A SUBSTITUTE

Some overenthusiastic pastors and leaders in Christian education have replaced the Sunday evening sermon with 16 mm. motion pictures. In some cases they have, perhaps unknowingly, turned the church service into a time of entertainment rather than a spiritual experience. This is a poor use of 16 mm. sound films. Occasional films do have their place in the regular services of the church, even in place of a sermon, but only when they are well chosen and used properly.

The following example illustrates correct use of a sound film in an evening church service: A church was planning to launch a visitation program to help reach the many new families moving into the community. Out of a discussion between the pastor and his assistant came the idea of renting a certain motion picture which would appeal to all age groups and challenge the church in its visitation responsibilities. The film was rented well in advance and publicized to be shown on a certain Sunday evening. When the day arrived, the pastor and his assistant met in the afternoon to preview the film. It was decided by both men, after the previewing, that the assistant should give a ten-minute talk to prepare the congregation for the message of the film. The pastor would prepare a fifteen-minute correlated message to follow up the film and challenge the people regarding visitation.[1] The service was outlined as follows:

7:45–7:50—Singing.

7:50–8:00—Preparation of the congregation by the assistant pastor.   (A brief synopsis of the film story was given; several points and incidents to look for during the showing were outlined.)

8:00–8:30—The film showing.

8:30–8:45—Correlated message by the pastor.

Due to the fact that this film was used correctly, the program was a success. A rewarding visitation program resulted.

Types and Values

Various types of motion pictures are available for use with children, young people, and adults and in all other areas of Christian education. It is impossible to avoid overlapping in classifying these films, but in general the following categories are practical (see Appendix II for film sources).

MISSIONARY FILMS

The 16 mm. motion-picture film has been very influential in promoting home and foreign missionary interest in the twentieth century. Prior to this marvelous invention, people were permitted merely to read, hear, but very seldom visualize reports of activity on the mission field. As a result, many did not enter into the prayer and financial burden as they should. Modern missionary films have brought the mission fields right into the churches and schools. Missionary activity at home and abroad can now be visualized by the majority of Christians. As a result many have been awakened to their responsibility to "go, or give and pray." Motion-picture films have not provided the answer for reaching the world's millions, but they have greatly aided in increasing missionary activity.

EVANGELISTIC FILMS

Evangelistic films, which are prepared particularly to present the message of salvation, have proved to be valuable in reaching people with the gospel of Christ. Evangelistic effort has been multiplied again and again by the showing of these effective films in areas where time, lack of facilities and religious prejudice prohibit an evangelist from going.

CHRISTIAN LIFE FILMS

Numerous 16 mm. films have been produced to challenge all ages to dedicate their lives to Christ in Christian living and service. True and fictional stories have been dramatized and produced by professionals. The main problem with these films is that they frequently do not measure up to the quality of secular productions. Since all ages of Americans are conditioned to view the best in motion pictures, a second-rate Christian film sometimes creates more negative than positive reactions.

LEADERSHIP TRAINING FILMS

Pastors, Sunday school teachers, youth leaders, and other laymen in the church are being challenged to do a more effective job with the use of leadership training films. These 16 mm. films are exceptionally valuable in that they demonstrate realistically how an effective Christian education program should be organized and administered.

BIBLE STORY FILMS

Outstanding Bible stories such as "Noah and the Ark," "David and Saul," "Daniel in the Lions' Den," and the "Life of Paul" are being produced on 16 mm. sound films. These films present dramatically and effectively the way God dealt with the people of old.

BIBLE-BACKGROUND FILMS

Subjects such as "How we got our Bible," and "How the Bible has been translated into many languages" have been treated dramatically. Other films depict geographical locations, ancient cities, and other interesting facts mentioned in Scripture, much of which has been made possible by recent archeological discoveries. These films are particularly helpful in aiding all ages to understanding the background and setting of the Bible and in illustrating the authenticity of the Scriptures.

PROMOTIONAL FILMS

Christian schools are preparing promotional films to attract young people. Life in a Bible institute or a Bible college is filmed, picturing the many aspects of school life. Many young people have experienced God's call to attend certain schools after seeing these films.

SCIENCE FILMS

Many science films present scientifically valid arguments for the existence of God and the reliability of the Bible as God's inspired revelation. These films have had a marvelous ministry all over the world. By means of telescopic and microscopic photography, the marvels of the universe have been portrayed on the screen, depicting outstanding evidence for the presence of God's creative hand.

DOCUMENTARY FILMS

A new type of film that has come into being in more recent years is the documentary—a news-type film. Designed to tell the facts about certain real-life situations, it contains a series of events with a descriptive commentary.

A number of secular documentaries have value for the church. For exam-

ple, films that present the youth culture are often well produced and lend
themselves to discussion, interaction and Christian interpretation. Sometimes a film of this nature can be more effective as a discussion starter than a
Christian film that attempts to present the facts as well as to present a Christian point of view.

Fig. 141. Bell and Howell 16 mm. projector

PROJECTORS

There are various types of 16 mm. sound projectors, and the majority of
them are constructed for long and effective use. As in the area of automobile
manufacturing, competition among the various companies making 16 mm.
projectors has helped to produce quality. Some machines, however, have
specially desirable features. It is wise to consult a specialist for comparison
before purchasing a machine, but it is generally true, as with any other type
of merchandise, that the higher the price, the better the quality and lasting
efficiency (see Figs. 141-43).

OPERATION

Many Christian workers are hesitant to attempt to use a 16 mm. motion-
picture projector because they believe its operation is too complicated and
that something might "go wrong." But anyone who can drive a car, run a

Fig. 142. Eastman Kodak 16 mm. projector

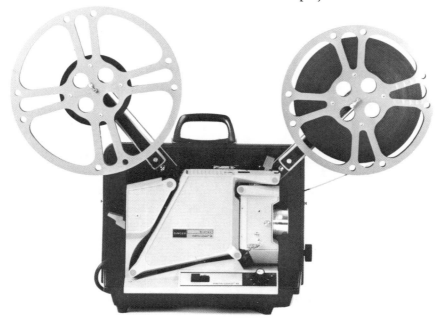

Fig. 143. Singer 16 mm. projector

sewing machine, or operate other modern and commonly used mechanical devices can operate a 16 mm. motion-picture projector. The operation, though it may seem to be involved, is relatively simple. A few rules of procedure are applicable in the use of most of these machines:

1. Set up the equipment by carefully following the instructions that come with the machine.

   a. Set up the speaker.

   b. Arrange the projector arms and take-up reel.

   c. Connect the cord with the electrical outlet (use AC only unless instructed otherwise).

   d. Clean the film gate with a small brush.

   e. Test the machine by turning on the motor and the lamp, and by turning up the volume and listening for a hiss or hum from the speaker.

2. Place the reel of film on the feed arm, and thread the projector.

   a. Make sure the film is wound correctly by checking the title.

   b. Check to see that the film is threaded correctly on the sprockets by rotating the hand control knob.

   c. Doublecheck by referring to the threading chart that accompanies the machine.

3. Start the machine. The following procedure should be used in setting up the equipment before the showing as well as during the actual showing of the film:

   a. Turn on the motor.

   b. Turn on the lamp.

   c. Fade in the volume.

   d. Adjust the tone.

   e. Check the framing and focus.

4. Check the film during the showing to make sure no damage is occurring.

   a. Gently touch the perforated edge of the film just before it goes on the take-up reel to make sure that the film is not being torn by the sprockets.

   b. If the film loops are lost, stop the projector and reform them. This problem is characterized by a blurred rush of pictures on the screen and a "clicking" noise.

5. Stop the projector after the showing.

   a. Turn off the lamp.

   b. Fade out the volume.

   c. Turn off the motor after the film has been run through the machine.

6. Put away the equipment and return the film to the library.

CARE

Every projector should be cared for periodically by an individual who knows about its intricate parts and their function. This will involve general lubrication, the replacing of defective lamps, fuses and belts, and the thorough cleaning of the lenses, reflector and film gate. If a major problem should arise, such as motor trouble, the machine should be returned to the dealer for special care. Most machines, if cared for in this manner, will operate effectively for many years.

Most common problems arise due to carelessness and lack of experience in operating the projector. Rare problems arise when the projector is not checked regularly, cared for properly, and when certain parts naturally wear out and need to be replaced. The projectionist's problem-finder that follows will help locate and overcome difficulties that may arise.[2]

PROJECTIONIST'S PROBLEM-FINDER

Problems	Common Causes	Uncommon Causes
Failure of projector to start	Line cord not connected Line cord not making contact	Blown fuse in building Loose connections
No sound	Amplifier not turned on Speaker not properly connected Volume not turned up	Defective exciter lamp Defective amplifier tubes Defective photo cell
Defective sound	Incorrect threading Incorrect speed Speaker placed in poor position	Damaged film Belts slipping
No picture	Projection lamp not turned on	Defective projection lamp
Poor picture	Lens out of focus Poor framing Incorrect speed Dirty lens or film channel Incorrect threading Room not darkened properly	Defective film Line cord not making proper contact Dirty reflector Belts slipping Low voltage Poor projection lamp alignment
Sound and picture not together	Incorrect threading	Poor film

Strange sounds	Loss of loops	Defective amplifier tubes
	Speaker improperly connected	Poor lubrication
	Improper threading	Defective exciter lamp
	Projector dirty	

PROJECTION SCREENS

In order to use projected pictures, it is necessary to have a projection screen. Various substitutes such as sheets, windows shades, and painted walls will do in an emergency, but every church should have a screen or several screens.

TYPES

Fig. 144. Rear projection screen (East-man Kodak)

The beaded screen and the matte screen are the most popular types. The beaded screen which is covered with small glass particles is a good buy. It reflects a brighter image than the matte screen and is particularly adaptable to rooms that are long and narrow. However, the matte screen is very usable. It permits a wider viewing angle, but the reflection is not as bright as that of the beaded screen. It is particularly good for use in a room that is wide with little depth.

Other screens that are available are silver and metallic screens, glass screens, rubber-backed screens, and also rear projection screens (see Fig. 144).

MODELS

Two models of screens are used most frequently. These are the portable tripod and the wall or ceiling screen (see Figs. 145-46). The portable tripod model is desirable in church situations. It can be quickly moved from room to room and can be stored easily. Large churches with many department rooms would do well to purchase some wall screens. They can be considered permanent fixtures in the rooms or some can be moved from room to room. Special brackets make this simple and economical (see Figs. 147-50).

Fig. 145. Da-Lite screen—a wall or ceiling screen

Fig. 146. A portable tripod screen

SIZES

Screen size is another important factor to consider. This is determined primarily by room size. A 70-by-70-inch screen mounted on a tripod is found to be applicable in most church situations. A smaller screen may be desired for class or department rooms, but even a larger screen than 70 by 70 inches may be desired for use in an auditorium.

PRODUCING FILMS

The production of 16 mm. films is a large subject and an area that requires professional abilities and highly developed skills. Some Christian organizations or individuals have attempted to produce films for various reasons only to find they have invested much money and have, as an end result, a poorly prepared film. It is not within the scope of this manual to suggest ideas for 16 mm. film production. It is advisable to seek professional help for this type of work.

However, many individuals are producing 8 mm. films for personal or family use. The cost is not prohibitive, and every interesting "home movies" can be prepared by the amateur photographer. Cameras and projectors can be purchased at the average photo supply shop. The development of the super 8 has added greatly to the quality of these productions.

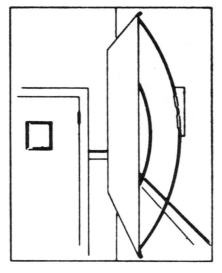

Fig. 147. Vertical position

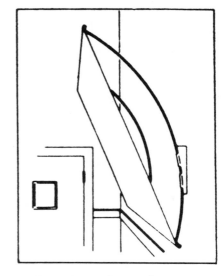

Fig. 148. Moderate tilt position

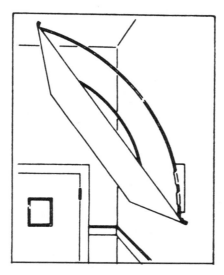

Fig. 149. Extreme tilt position

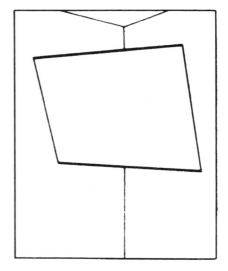

Fig. 150. Corner mounting

An inexpensive specialized screen shown here provides permanent classroom mounting and is adjustable for all types of projection. Especially adaptable for overhead projection (Technifax Corp.)

When revising this chapter on motion pictures, I saw an article written by Glen Arnold in which he tells a story that includes so many unique ideas and principles that I'm including the entire article at the close of this chapter:

How to Produce a Children's Film Without Actually Crying

The lights in the sanctuary dimmed, the rumble of the timpani began to build a crescendo through the public-address system, and members of the children's church staff tensed. Then there it was in pulsating hues on the seventy by seventy-inch screen in the chancel— our Children's Day production in super-eight color, "The Good Samaritan"!

This moment—so exhilarating for both children and adults—climaxed nine months of dreaming, planning and producing by the children's church of the First Baptist Church of Park Ridge, Illinois.

"Why, if I had known what this film was going to be like," enthused one mother, "I would have brought my neighbors. Why didn't you tell me?"

To such a question there was only one answer. "Not even those of us who had been working on the project for months really knew what the final product would be," commented Dorothy Crane, junior church director. "This was a first-time experience for adults as well as children."

The idea had first gripped both the youngsters and their elders when Dennis Shippy, a communications major at Moody Bible Institute, showed a film he had directed and produced in his home church when he was in high school. Using an eight-millimeter camera he had purchased from a dime store, he and the young people of his church had created an impressive film on Christ's nativity.

A showing of Dennis' film to the children's church staff and to the board of Christian education pushed everyone involved across the bridge of uncertainty. They had been hooked on a 400-foot line of celluloid!

The first step was to ask the children if they would be interested in a film project. Their enthusiastic affirmative left no doubt as to their feeling.

The staff, concerned that the children participate from the beginning, next asked them what Bible story they wanted to present.

"Jesus walking on the water!"

"Noah and the ark!"

After explaining as diplomatically as possible that these first suggestions might involve technical difficulties, Curt Pinnell, primary church director, suggested that the children research in Bible-story books so they could see for themselves some of the physical problems involved in recreating their favorites. This research, done in small groups using Bibles and books from the church library, led to the children's choice of the parable of the Good Samaritan.

Further study followed. First the account in Luke was read in a number of translations and versions. Pictures of the dress and houses in first-century

Palestine were carefully observed. Drawings were made of costumes, designs for the inn and murals of outdoor scenes. Donna Wadsworth, a dramatically oriented high schooler, assisted in writing a script.

Solomon's wisdom was needed for the next step. Which children should take the leading roles? In general, the children agreed to the suggestion that the oldest be given such leading parts as the victim, the good Samaritan, the Levite and the innkepeer. Eventually each child had at least one part although from the standpoint of numbers the way to Jericho looked more like a modern interstate highway than a lonely road!

Pleas went out through the church paper, by phone and through the children themselves for help in collecting the needed properties and costumes. A flood of bathrobes, scarfs, sandals and towels poured into the Christian education office with many parents wondering what kind of rummage sale the staff was running now.

Rehearsals began indoors during the winter as part of the weekly program with the children practicing according to the scenes. At the same time, boys and girls on the art staff began drawing murals of what they thought the outdoor and inn settings should look like.

One adult leader suggested that the road scenes be shot outdoors instead of against a mural, and a tour of a nearby forest preserve quickly revealed an ideal setting complete with a huge boulder—a perfect hiding place for the attackers!

Early in the spring after one or two fresh-air rehearsals, the outdoor scenes were filmed. These were completed in three weeks. The attack incident was filmed from a number of angles and was acted out so enthusiastically that leaders were relieved to see the victim get up by himself. The emerging foliage and the progressive deepening of the green hues as the weeks passed gave the producers some uneasy moments, but these problems were largely unnoticed in the final film.

The stage in the church's Fellowship Hall made a good location for filming the inn scenes. All went smoothly here with the exception of the appearance of a very modern light switch at the inn's entrance and an over-zealous innkeeper and his wife who nearly suffocated the attack victim under a mound of blankets.

Editing was the most traumatic step for the adult staff. For several weeks, the Christian education office was decorated with dozens of strips of super-eight film along the walls, each identified as to scene. Previously, not one of the adult leaders had done any film editing beyond work on home movies.

After initial help from the Bible school student, staff members found themselves on their own in their attempt to get the right section of film, at the appropriate time, in the correct place.

Background music was transferred to a master tape and by means of the "add-a-track" feature on the church's tape recorder, the narration and taped background of children's voices were added. Making the tape took several evenings.

As each roll of film came back from the camera shop, it was shown to the children the following Sunday. Interest was high. Finally on the Sunday before Children's Day the film in nearly complete form was presented at the children's church service. The children's enthusiastic response forecast a sanctuary overflowing with parents and friends one week later.

The Children's Day program became a double feature because each major step had been filmed and several cassette recordings had been made as the children worked on their project. These activities provided footage for feature one, "The Making of a Movie," a twenty-minute documentary of the previous nine months' activity in children's church. Then, following announcements and offering, "The Good Samaritan" was shown for fifteen minutes to an appreciative and enthusiastic congregation.

Some had been concerned about showing the films in the sanctuary. In fact adult leaders had found themselves praying for a cloudy day so that the pictures would have a brighter image on the screen. These prayers were answered in the form of a cloudburst shortly before service time. Though advance preparation had been made to darken the sanctuary by masking some of the windows, the heavenly help made it possible for everyone to see clearly.

What does it cost to produce a mini-spectacular? By borrowing cameras, lights and projectors from adult members, expenses were held to $150 of the $200 set aside in the budget. Most of that amount went to pay for film and processing.

Does this seem expensive? When the benefits and values of the project were considered most of those involved agree that it was a small and very worthwhile investment. The teaching value of the project was recognized by all. The children who made the film and the parents who saw it received new insights into the parable. Each child was asked what the story meant to him.

In addition the children were given many opportunities for self-expression through writing, drawing, painting, planning and acting, all with focus on the Bible's teaching. The participants also learned teamwork. Finally, the church now has its own uniquely effective film of the Good Samaritan parable for use in Sunday school, children's church and vacation Bible school.

While there were times when tears might have been used instead of splicing tape or glue to splice the film, yet almost everyone—children, adults and youth—agree that the total effort was one of the richest Christian education experiences the church has ever offered.[3]

Discussion Questions

1. What can you relate regarding an unusually successful film showing which you have experienced? What made it successful?

2. What poor film showing have you experienced? Why was this the case? How could it have been improved?

Special Projects

1. View a good motion picture that can be used in the church program. As a group, discuss the possible ways of getting the most effective use from the film (teacher preparation, group preparation, follow-up, etc.).

2. Practice operating a motion-picture projector until you can do it quickly and easily. Use the instructions given on p. 168 as a checklist.

3. Become very familiar with the common causes of projector problems which are charted on pp. 169-70.

4. Prepare a sample checklist which could be used in training others to operate the motion-picture projector.

5. If accessible, spend some time previewing several sound films that are available for use in the church program.

6. Use a super 8 camera and projector and prepare a film presentation, using a tape recorder to provide audio effects.

11

Filmstrips and 2-by-2-Inch Slides

NUMEROUS FILMSTRIPS are available for use in Christian education. In each filmstrip there are normally twenty to fifty frames (see Fig. 151). Each filmstrip is kept in a small metal or plastic container. Each container may be stored in a small metal filing cabinet prepared especially for easy location (see Fig. 152).

Most filmstrips are accompanied by written scripts, records or tape recordings. Others may have the script included right on the projected frame. If records or tape recordings accompany the filmstrips, they are called sound filmstrips. The records usually include narration with appropriate music which may be played on a record player. Most records are now being prepared at 33 1/3 rpm. due to the large amount of narration that can be put on one side. This makes for smooth presentation, avoiding the interruptions that come when records have to be turned over or changed. The content of tape recordings is like that of records, and they may be played on a standard machine at 3¾ ips. or 7½ ips. or on a cassette recorder.

The 2-by-2-inch slides are transparent pictures mounted individually and projected by a light which passes through the film and lens onto the screen. They are ordinarily mounted in cardboard or plastic.

Especially prepared slides may be purchased from various evangelical film producers; however, anyone can easily take his own colored pictures with a 35 mm. camera. Missionaries especially find great value in taking colored slides. When the films are being processed, they are mounted in cardboard and come back in the form of "ready mounts" which may be immediately inserted into the projector. They may be kept in special containers or files ready for immediate use (see Fig. 153).

Fig. 152. Filmstrip cabinet (Wilson)

Fig. 153. Slide file (Barnett and Jaffe)

TYPES AND VALUES OF FILMSTRIPS

There are many different types of filmstrips prepared to meet various needs. The major types are leadership training, Bible story, and missionary filmstrips.

The area of "leadership training" is worthy of particular emphasis. Many excellent filmstrips are being produced to help train people to take their place of responsibility in the work of Christian education. Where the general principles for using projected aids are applied in the use of these filmstrips, the results in terms of increased leadership ability are remarkable (see Fig. 154).

Commercially made 2-by-2-inch slides are not prepared for as extensive a program as filmstrips and they are more expensive to purchase. Many are limited to Bible background and biblical scenes. The greatest value of 2-by-2-inch slides is found in the opportunity for Christian workers to prepare their own with a 35 mm. camera.

Fig. 154. Filmstrips lend themselves well for use in small groups, particularly in the area of leadership training (Singer)

Although filmstrips and slides lack the great advantage of motion, they have some advantages over 16 mm. sound films. Three of the more important advantages are:

MORE NUMEROUS

Filmstrips which will easily fit into particular units of study are being produced more rapidly than 16 mm. sound films.

LESS EXPENSIVE

Fig. 155. Preview filmstrips before purchasing as well as before using them (Standard)

Filmstrips and slides are usually purchased rather than rented. Since the cost of production is less expensive, filmstrips and slides can be purchased more cheaply than most motion-picture films can be rented.

In addition, filmstrips and slides become a permanent part of the audiovisual library, available for use again and again, year after year, as they are worked into curriculum units. However, a word of warning is in order; since they become permanent property of the church, they need to be selected carefully. Not all filmstrips and slides will make a satisfactory contribution to the program of Christian education (see Fig. 155).

MORE VERSATILE

Filmstrips and 2-by-2-inch slides make up for lack of motion by their flexibility. They allow for much variation in their use and provide opportunities for discussion during the actual presentation. Furthermore, the equipment is easier to move about, set up and operate (see Fig. 156).

Fig. 156. Filmstrip and slide equipment is easy to move about, set up and operate (Eastman Kodak)

THE COMBINATION FILMSTRIP AND SLIDE PROJECTORS

The combination filmstrip and slide projector is a valuable tool in Christian education, for it has a dual ministry. Separate units which show either filmstrips or 2-by-2-inch slides may be purchased, but there is a consistent need for the use of both filmstrips and slides. A combination machine can project both (see Figs. 157-58).

There are certain definite characteristics to look for in purchasing this type of machine:

1. It should be simple in operation.

2. It should project a brilliant image (a 300- or 500-watt lamp is usually satisfactory).

3. It should project a good-sized picture the length of the classroom or auditorium. (A 5-inch lens is satisfactory in most situations. For exceptionally long-range projections, a 7-inch lens may be needed.)

4. It should have an effective cooling system, preferably the type with a fan.

The following rules are applicable in operating most machines of this type:

Fig. 157. Viewlex Projector ready for filmstrip viewing

Fig. 158. Standard projector ready for slide projection

To Show Filmstrips

1. Read the operating instructions carefully. Some machines are operated manually while some work with a push-button control; also, some machines are equipped for automatic projection, using an electronically recorded signal on a record or tape.

2. Remove the equipment from the carrying case (not always necessary).

3. Make sure the filmstrip unit is in place.

4. Remove the filmstrip from the container.

5. Check the title to make sure the filmstrip is wound correctly (most machines thread from the outside of the roll).

6. Place the filmstrip in the holder on the machine and push the filmstrip into the projector.

7. Turn the knob on the machine to pull the filmstrip through the projector.

8. Turn on the lamp.

9. Frame and focus the picture on the screen.

10. Set up the record player if a record accompanies the filmstrip.

11. Synchronize the record or reading script with the proper frame.

Fig. 159. Standard

Fig. 160. Viewlex

Fig. 161. Standard

Fig. 162. Viewlex

To Show 2-by-2-Inch Slides

1. Read the operating instructions carefully.

2. Remove the filmstrip unit from the machine (this is not necessary on all types).

3. Make sure slide-changer or unit is in place.

4. Turn on the lamp.

5. Insert slide into the slide-changer and move slide-changer until the picture is projected on the screen.

6. Focus the picture.

THE COMBINATION FILMSTRIP PROJECTOR AND RECORD PLAYER

Since many filmstrips are accompanied by a disk recording, it is wise to consider purchasing a filmstrip projector that is equipped with a record player. This type of machine is especially useful when the recording is prepared with an inaudible signal designed to change filmstrip frames automatically (see Figs. 159-62).

Some of the most popular machines of this type are produced by the Dukane Corporation. There is one important thing to keep in mind when using the Dukane projector: *Remember that the filmstrip feeds into the machine from the inside of the filmstrip roll* (see Fig. 163).

COMBINING SLIDES AND TAPE

It is possible to prepare a slide presentation with your own tape-recorded narration. Equipment is available to record a sound signal on one track of a stereo recorder so the slides will change automatically.

For example, a Kodak Carousel Sound Synchronizer is ideal for synchronizing a stereo tape recording with projectors with remote-control outlets. During the recording session, the sound is taped on one track, and a signal is recorded on the second track. When you play the recording, the signal you have recorded on the second track will advance the projector automatically. Furthermore, if you wish to change your signals, you simply redo the recording (see Fig. 164).

MULTIPLE-PROJECTOR AND MULTIPLE-SCREEN PRESENTATIONS

Excellent equipment is now available to produce presentations using two or more projectors and two or more screens (see Fig. 165). In some instances you may wish to use only one screen but two projectors, fading from one picture to another. In this way the screen is never "black," but the slides are dissolved from one to the other. As one slide fades out, another slide from the second projector fades onto the screen. Though you are using

Fig. 163. Using the Dukane projector. Note: It is important to notice that the filmstrip feeds into the projector from inside the roll on the Dukane. (Dukane)

Fig. 164. Recording a signal on a second track of a stereo recorder so that the slides will advance automatically when the recording is played back (Eastman Kodak)

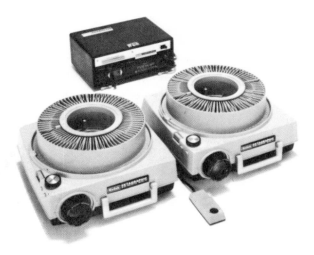

Fig. 165. Utilizing two projectors in a slide presentation (Eastman Kodak)

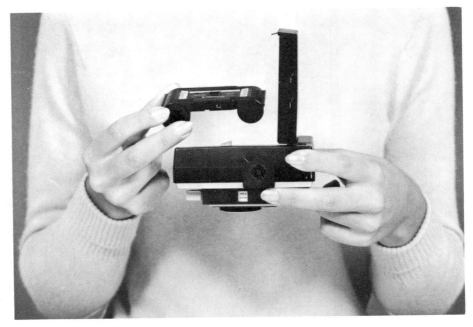

Fig. 166. Inserting a color film cartridge into a Kodak instamatic camera

Fig. 167. Inserting a flash cube for indoor pictures

"still" pictures, the effect of fading will in some instances give the sensation of "motion."

You may also wish to superimpose one picture over another, or do a multiple-screen presentation. When you use two or more screens, you have a variety of possibilities. You may wish to have all screens filled with pictures at the same time, or you can use only one screen part of the time. You may also desire to have a motion picture on one of the screens.

One word of caution: In designing a multiple-screen presentation, make sure that communication is enhanced rather than hindered. It is possible to have so much happening that the only real value to the audience is an "electric experience" in sight and sound. The verbal message is lost in a conglomerate of sensations, leaving the person with an existential experience, but no concrete message.

PREPARING A SLIDE PRESENTATION

Not too many years ago, it required a lot of photographic background and skill to take good 2-by-2-inch slides. Today, however, 35 mm. cameras have been simplified to such an extent that all a person need do is insert a film cartridge in the camera, press the shutter release, and take a picture. A built-in light meter automatically sets the lens opening. And if you use a single lens reflex camera, you can see in advance what the final picture will actually look like (see Figs. 166-69).

Fig. 168. A built-in light meter makes no lense adjustments necessary for either indoor or outdoor pictures (Eastman Kodak)

Fig. 169. Making color slides with the Kodak visual maker. All you need to do is press the shutter release. No settings are necessary. (Eastman Kodak)

There is, of course, the more sophisticated approach to slide-taking, using a system of lenses and other techniques. The end product will naturally be more outstanding.

GUIDING PRINCIPLES FOR TAKING GOOD SLIDES

Randomly aiming a camera at a variety of objects and pushing the shutter release will not necessarily result in a good slide series. Nor will it result in "good" slides. A "colorful picture" with proper exposure is not synonymous with a "good" slide.

Slide-taking involves composition: those elements you include in each individual picture and the way in which those elements are related to each other. To develop a good "series" means having a number of individual slides with proper composition that will fit together in an appropriate sequence to tell a basic story or to present an overall idea.

Here are some suggestions for accomplishing these objectives:

1. Prepare a "picture-taking roadmap"—a shooting schedule. If possible, prepare a rough draft of a script which will serve as this "roadmap."

2. Take interesting pictures. Be "choosy" about subjects. Take several shots of one scene from various angles. This will enable you to select the best pictures for your final presentation, and will make it possible for you to use "picture sequence." For example, you may take a picture of a group of people, but as the sequence continues you can show closeups of certain individuals in the group.

3. Strive to have a center of interest; however, it should not be exactly in the center of the picture but slightly above or below and to either side of the exact center.

4. Unless you are a skilled photographer with rather sophisticated equipment, take pictures in the sunlight during the period between two hours after sunrise and two hours before sunset. For even better results, the hours before ten in the morning and after three in the afternoon will help avoid shadows that are caused from the sun being directly overhead. (Note: A skilled photographer actually makes use of bad weather to enhance his slide series.[1]

5. Try to avoid having people pose for pictures. Take natural, spontaneous shots. To get good pictures, however, you will need to introduce a certain amount of "subject control." For example, include frames of arches, a fence, or branches from a tree. You can also include other objects in the foreground, such as people wearing bright sweaters or jackets. If there are no trees or bushes, have someone hold a tree branch in front of your lens.

Eliminate items that may spoil your pictures—such as trash—from the foreground, unless this is part of your composition.

Don Nibbelink has suggested some interesting techniques for "subject control," when photographing various objects:[2]

a. When photographing flowers, splash a few drops of water on the petals to make your own "dew."

b. When photographing animals, use sound, food incentives, enclosed areas, and other techniques to create unusual expressions.

c. Put people at ease; use one-line jokes; have them perform some activity; but don't have them look at the camera.

6. To develop your photographic skills, consult literature that will give you more in-depth knowledge. For example, the Eastman Kodak Company has prepared a series of excellent *Here's How* booklets, covering information on exposure meters, lenses, nature photography, photographing children, animals, underwater photography, etc.

GUIDING PRINCIPLES FOR PREPARING A SLIDE SERIES

1. Lay out your exposed slides on a "slide illuminator." If you already have a rough script, group your slides according to the sequence of ideas.

2. Select the best slides for use in your presentation. Don't make your final choices until you've actually seen them projected on a screen.

3. Decide on captions and other art work you may wish to include in the slide presentation. These slides will need to be shot separately.

4. Finalize the script by writing it or rewriting it in direct relationship to the pictures you will be projecting on the screen. (Note: In some instances, the final script should emerge from the inductive process of selecting and organizing the slides into an acceptable sequence.)

5. Make sure you use a lot of slides, not to create a long presentation, but so that they move quickly. Slides should seldom be left on the screen more than a few seconds. In a fifteen-minute presentation you can easily show 100 to 150 slides.

PREPARING A FILMSTRIP

It is usually not a wise procedure to produce a filmstrip unless you plan to make multiple copies and circulate them widely. All of the steps just described regarding the production of a 2-by-2-inch slide series, are also necessary in producing a filmstrip. It is important, however, that very careful steps are taken in order to produce slides that can be copied and made into an acceptable filmstrip.

The same is true of a sound track. Before a taped sound track is permanently pressed and made into a disk recording, it should be as perfect as possible. Thus it is advisable to employ a team of photographic and recording experts to produce filmstrips.

SPECIAL PROJECTS

1. View a 35 mm. filmstrip and a set of 2-by-2-inch slides. As a group, discuss the most effective ways they can be used in the church.

2. Prepare your own slide series, applying the suggestions and principles included in this chapter.

3. Try your hand at a multimedia production, using two or more projectors or screens.

12

Recordings

Tape recordings are very useful with all age groups and can help Christian workers do a more effective job in all areas of Christian education. Once the many values of this audio-aid are discovered, every church will gladly make the investment.

DESCRIPTION

Reel-to-reel recorders. There are many different makes and types of tape recorders, and most of them are not overly expensive. They are easily moved from room to room, simple to operate, and the reproduction on most common types is of good quality.

Most portable reel-to-reel recorders operate at three speeds: $1\frac{7}{8}$ inches per second, $3\frac{3}{4}$ inches per second, and $7\frac{1}{2}$ inches per second. The majority of dual-track machines will record on half of the tape the first time through and, when the tape is reversed, they will record on the second half. A single-track machine, which is primarily for use on radio, will record only on one area of the tape (see Figs. 170-172).

Many tape recorders are designed to record two tracks simultaneously, thus producing stereophonic sound. The stereo system contains two separate recording heads which pick up sound through microphones in two separate locations. During the playback, this sound is reproduced through two loud speakers placed in two separate locations, just as the microphones were spaced apart during the recording session. Consequently, you experience a realistic effect, referred to as a "live" listening experience. The sound

191

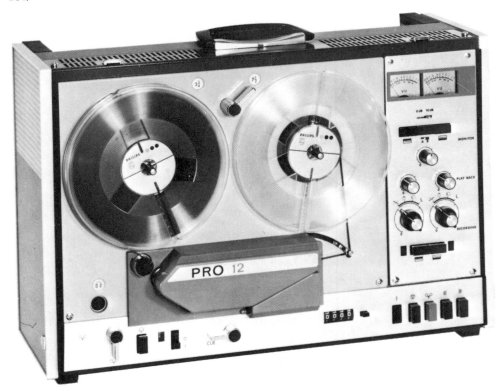

Fig. 170. Norelco recorder

Fig. 171. Sony recorder

Fig. 172. Rheem Califone

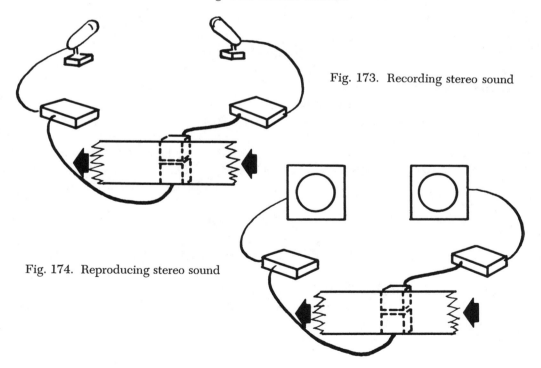

Fig. 173. Recording stereo sound

Fig. 174. Reproducing stereo sound

reaches your ears as if you were listening to an orchestra or group of singers actually performing (see Figs. 173-74).

When purchasing a reel-to-reel recorder for your church, consider purchasing a stereo machine, which is recommended due to its versatility and multiple use:

1. It can be used by the choir to realistically record their practice sessions for later evaluation.

2. It can be used in the church auditorium, and in department and classrooms for listening to stereo music.

3. It can also be used to play single-track recordings.

4. It can be used to record special programs and unique sound productions where a stereo effect will enhance the recording.

5 It can be used to produce sound-slide presentations where a sound synchronizer is used to change the slides automatically. (See pp. 184-5).

Cassette recorders. Tape cassettes represent a remarkable breakthrough in tape recording. Even more significant, this tool has opened the door for unusual opportunities in Christian education. Statistics show that people have purchased more cassette recorders than record players. They have "invaded the home, the automobile, the school and the church" (see Figs. 175-77).

Cassette equipment is inexpensive, light-weight, portable, and usually operates on both batteries or regular electric power. Some machines are equipped with built-in microphones with automatic leveling devices, a real advantage when recording group conferences, class discussions, and even sermons. The cassette mike will pick up sound very well from regular loud speakers, adjusting itself accordingly.

One problem with the automatic leveling mike is that if you are recording a voice some distance away, and you are surrounded by people who are coughing, shuffling their feet, and scraping chairs, the mike will adjust to these noises first, and consequently cut the recording level down so that the sounds you are primarily after are not recorded effectively (see Fig. 178).

Cassette recordings provide these unusual opportunities for Christian education:

1. They can be used for repeated listening—in a classroom, at home, in the car as you travel—in short, almost anywhere.

2. They can be used by individuals for self-study purposes—in a "listening corner" in the church library, or in a Sunday school department learning center (headphones are ideal for this purpose).

3. They can be used to record class and small-group discussion, for use in evaluating the session, for immediate playback and review, for sharing with other groups, etc.

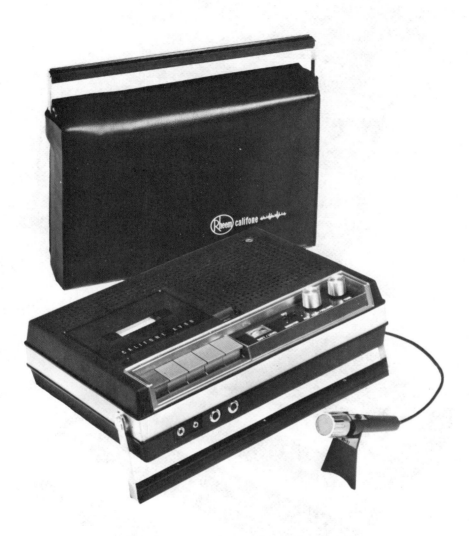

Fig. 175. Rheem Califone cassette recorder

Fig. 176. Bell and Howell cassette recorder

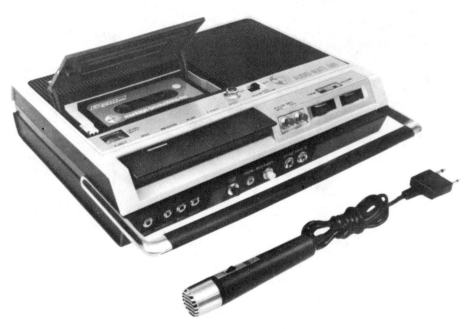

Fig. 177. Montage Audio-Mate cassette recorder

Fig. 178. Cassette recorders are easily transported and can be used under a variety of circumstances.

4. They can be used to do telephone tape recordings for use in the classroom (Note: Be sure to inform the person whose voice you are recording and seek his permission to use the telephone tape in your class).

5. They can be used effectively on a circulating basis to communicate with missionaries, neighbors, friends, hospitalized people, etc.

Tapes. Most tapes for reel-to-reel recorders are made with a plastic base and may be purchased in several different lengths. The most common lengths are 600 and 1,200 feet.

Recordings on tapes may be preserved indefinitely and used many times if they are kept in a storage place where the temperature is moderate and even and where the humidity is low. An average room is usually satisfactory. These recordings may also be erased and the tape used over again for new recordings. Tapes may be used hundreds of times without affecting the quality of the recording.

Tape cassettes are small cartridges that fit into the cassette recorders. They record on the upper and lower sections of the tape, allowing you to flip the cartridge over. Cassettes come in varying lengths, the average ranging from thirty minutes to two hours of recording time on a single cartridge (see Fig. 179).

SELECTING TAPE RECORDERS

The following points will aid in selecting a tape recorder for home or church use:

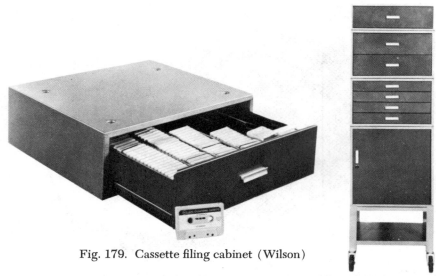

Fig. 179. Cassette filing cabinet (Wilson)

1. Talk to various people who have already purchased tape recorders, getting their reactions regarding the machines they have used.

2. Consider the quality of the recorder before considering the price. Many times a low-priced machine will cost more over a period of time due to mechanical failures. As with other types of audiovisual equipment, the quality corresponds with the cost.

3. Look for a machine that has a minimum of buttons and knobs but one that does an effective job.

4. Select a recorder that is equipped with a footage meter or other device for tape measurement. This will enable the person who is using the machine to quickly find certain spots on the tape. For example, a musical group may be preparing a recording. The machine starts recording at number fifty. As soon as the song has been completed it is a simple matter to reverse the tape to number fifty, the exact spot where the recording began.

5. Select a recorder that is easy to set up, operate, and move from place to place.

6. Select a recorder that has a fast forward and rewind speed.

7. When selecting a reel-to-reel machine, select one that will use reels of tape up to at least seven inches in size.

8. Select a recorder that is complete in one unit. The exception to this rule would be if a high-quality machine is purchased for radio broadcasting. In that case a two-unit machine may be desired.

9. Select a reel-to-reel recorder that operates at three speeds ($1\frac{7}{8}$, $3\frac{3}{4}$, and $7\frac{1}{2}$ inches per second). The slower speed will be satisfactory for recording speech and will allow twice the time for recording. The faster speed

should be used for music, since the faster tape speed provides better reproduction.

The following steps will apply in the operation of most reel-to-reel tape recorders, though the instructions that come with each make should always be consulted:

1. Place the recorder in a convenient place. It may be operated from the floor but is easier to use from a table or a desk.

2. Remove the cover and plug the electric cord into an AC socket. Turn on the amplifier.

3. Place the reel of tape on the side marked "feed reel" and the empty reel on the side marked "take-up reel." (Not all machines are marked.)

4. Unroll about one foot of tape from the full reel and thread the tape into the machine onto the empty spool.

5. Make sure the knob or button is adjusted for "playing" if the tape already contains a recording that is to be played back and is not to be erased. Also make sure the machine is set for the proper speed. Adjust the volume and tone as desired.

6. If a new recording is to be made on the tape, plug in the microphone (or microphones) on a stereo machine and set in a convenient place. Microphones should be placed some distance away from the machine so that they will not pick up machine noises. Set the machine for the desired speed. If an exceptional recording is desired, make sure there are no noises such as running motors, car horns, footsteps, scraping chairs, coughing, etc.

7. Experiment before attempting the final recording. Place the microphones in various positions and adjust the volume control knobs until the desired reproduction is obtained.

8. Start recording immediately, even if a previous recording has been made on the tape. It is not necessary to run the tape completely through the recorder so as to erase the previous recording before making a new one. The erasing is done automatically as the new recording is put on the tape.

9. Set the machine for "rewind" after the recording has been made and run the tape back onto the original reel. Adjust the "play back" knobs and the recording can be played back immediately.

10. Splice the tape if it breaks. This can be done easily by using the special Scotch splicing tape no. 41 as illustrated in Figures 180-84. Overlap the two broken ends and cut the pieces diagonally. Lay the two ends together with the shiny side up on a plastic base tape or the gray side up on a paper base tape. Place a piece of Scotch splicing tape over the cut and press securely. Trim the edges.

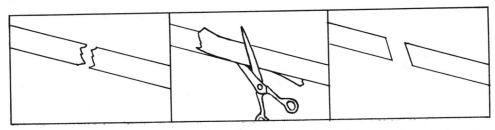

Fig. 180. A broken tape   Fig. 181. Overlap and cut   Fig. 182. Align both ends
tape at an angle   of the tape

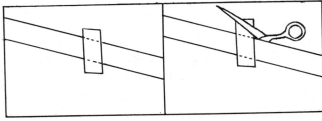

Fig. 183. Cover ends with Scotch splicing   Fig. 184. Cut off extending ends of the
tape. Make sure the shiny side is up.   splicing tape. Trim the edges very
                                              closely so that edges are not left
                                              on the tape.

11. Edit a recording by removing a section of the tape and splicing it together or by erasing. (Note: You cannot edit material on a multitrack recording since you will destroy part of the second recording.)

12. Clean the playing and recording heads by using a piece of soft fabric wrapped on a small stick. Use a regular cleaning fluid prepared for cleaning mechanical parts on recorders, projectors, and other audiovisual equipment.

USING RECORDERS

There are many opportunities for using tape recorders in Christian education. Following are some suggestions, in addition to those already mentioned in relationship to cassettes:

To accompany visual aids. Every teacher can provide his own recorded sound effects to be used with many different types of nonprojected and projected visual aids. In addition, many interesting group projects can be originated.

1. Aids for leaders. Some teaching filmstrips are accompanied by tape-recorded narration. If this is the case, they need to be placed on the recorder, and the sound synchronized with the filmstrips. But most filmstrips may be purchased much more inexpensively without sound, with only the printed

manual which includes the narration. It is a very simple process for Christian leaders to provide their own audio-narration by reading the script found in the manual and recording it on tape. There is also the possibility of providing an original narration with additional sound effects to accompany filmstrips, slides, and overhead projections (see Figs. 185-86).

Instead of using the flannelboard as usual, Christian workers will succeed in creating greater interest and in adding variety to their teaching by recording the narration and by adding music and other sound effects. Posters or a series of pictures may be used in a similar manner.

Leaders with artistic ability who present "chalk talks" may also make use of tape recorders. Recordings of music, narration, and additional sound effects may be prepared for playing while they are drawing. An excellent repertoire of beautiful and graphic recordings can soon be made for use with a number of different scenes.

Tape recordings may be used effectively for audiovisual publicity purposes. A recorder playing an especially prepared message accompanied by an appropriate poster will create unusual interest. Also, tape-recorded sound effects for use with 8 mm. movies taken at last year's camp, youth retreat, or vacation Bible school will add variety to the publicity program (see pp. 171-75).

2. Group projects. All ages will enjoy the opportunities provided for participation in group projects when tape recorders and visual aids are used. Children will enjoy preparing a flannelboard lesson, a series of still pictures or a slide presentation to be used with their own recorded sound effects. With careful guidance, children can make puppets and produce a puppet play with a recorded script. As the recording plays, they will have freedom to manipulate the puppets, and the problem of memorizing parts will also be alleviated. Even young people and leaders enjoy producing puppet plays for use with children.

The tape recorder may be used with actual dramatic productions. The script can be recorded on tape, and the actors will provide the action by pantomime as the tape is being played. This method has been used numerous times with great success. Special kits presenting the Christmas, Easter and other Bible stories are easily prepared. Additional stories such as *Pilgrim's Progress* and Christian fiction make excellent productions (see Fig. 187).

To be used alone. Tape recorders may also be used to provide sound without the use of visual aids. To add variety, teachers may occasionally record their own Bible stories, songs, and other instructional activities. A continued story may be used very effectively.

1. Radio programs. If a Christian broadcasting station is being operated

Fig. 185. Combination cassette-filmstrip recorder (Standard)

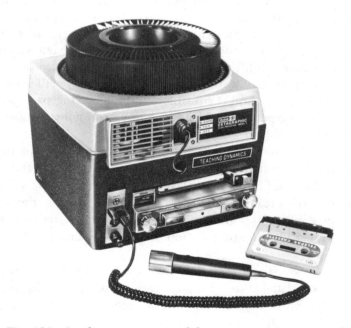

Fig. 186. Combination cassette-slide projector (Eastman Kodak)

Fig. 187. Various techniques can be used for making good recordings—here a sound box assists in controlling sound. (Eastman Kodak)

in the area, Bible stories, songs and special programs may be recorded directly from the radio for use with all age groups. These may be used effectively in Sunday schools, clubs, youth meetings and other agencies of Christian education.

2. Communication. There are various ways to use tape recorders to communicate with others. Sermons, song services, and other special programs may be recorded to be played for shut-ins. Young people's groups will find inspiration from taping their meetings and exchanging them with youth groups in other parts of the country. One of the most valuable opportunities provided by tape recorders is that of being able to communicate with missionaries in foreign lands.

3. Self-improvement. Pastors evangelists, missionaries, Sunday school teachers, musicians, and all other Christian workers need to improve their verbal presentations. Tape recorders provide this opportunity without embarrassment. Listening to one's own speaking or singing voice is revealing; areas which need improvement are easily detected. For an interesting experiment, keep the first tape made of the voice; after working to improve quality, enunciation, inflection, etc., make another recording on a second tape and compare the two.

4. Group improvement. A music director will also find excellent assistance from the tape recorder which will help to improve the choir, orchestra, and the other musical groups in the church. Careful recording will reveal proper or improper balance, pitch, expression and enunciation.

RECORDS

Disk recordings have provided hours of enjoyable listening for many people for many years. Some homes contain huge record collections of all types of musical recordings. Many individuals have not hesitated to invest large sums of money in order to purchase high-fidelity phonographs to provide the best in listening.

In addition to musical recordings which are having a wide ministry in the home and the church, records have been prepared specifically for use in Christian education. As mentioned previously, most narrations and other audio effects that accompany filmstrips are now being produced on 33 1/3 rpm. records. In addition to these excellent audiovisual aids, disk recordings alone may be obtained for use in the church. Some of these include children's story and song records. Records for learning foreign languages are being used by students preparing for Christian work. Records are also available to teach Bible survey and doctrinal courses.

Excellent disk recordings which deserve special mention are those which have been made of the Bible. Records of entire books of the Bible are available. Scripture passages are read with expression and careful enunciation. These records are exceptionally helpful for older people who can no longer read well and for people of all ages who are blind but who are able to hear (many of these records are also available on cassettes).

In the area of audio-disk recordings there is a continuing supply of good instructional material. More records that correlate with curriculum units are being produced, although cassette recordings will no doubt replace disk recordings used for this purpose. Every church should be able to build a library of records that may be used in all areas of its work (see Appendix II).

RECORD PLAYERS

Selection. A record player that is purchased for the church should be a three- or four-speed player (78, 45, 33 1/3 and 16 2/3 rpm.). It should be a portable machine, but one that has good fidelity (see Figs. 188-90).

Operation. The following points will aid in the use of a record player:

1. Place the machine so that the speaker (or speakers) is about even with the ears of the listeners.

2. Make sure that everyone is able to hear clearly. Experiment by listening from all areas of the room.

3. Handle records carefully. Take hold of the edges to avoid leaving fingerprints and scratches. Use a special record brush to clean the lint and dust from the recordings before they are used.

4. Use a microgroove needle for long-playing records (45 and 33 1/3

Fig. 188. Califone Model 1450B

Fig. 189. Califone Model 1815

Fig. 190. Califone Model 1865A

rpm.) or the disks will be damaged. The finer grooves on these records require a finer needle. Most good three- or four-speed machines are equipped with this type.

5. Keep the player in good repair. Never play records with a damaged or worn-out needle.

USING RECORDS IN CHRISTIAN EDUCATION

Opportunities for use. Disk recordings may be used for presession activity. Children will enjoy listening to stories and songs. Use records to add variety in worship services and instructional sessions. Correlate them well with curriculum units.

Records may be used for all ages in teaching songs. They provide opportunities with children in the Sunday school, vacation Bible school, weekday church school, etc. Choirs, quartets, trios and other special musical groups will receive beneficial help from listening to records of the musical numbers they are learning.

Many pastors and other Christian workers have found musical recordings very effective in small rural churches and meetings where talent is scarce. Organ music and other types may be used for preludes, offertories, special numbers and postludes.

Some churches find records very effective in producing radio programs. Rather than using their own talent, they use professional gospel musicians. By special permission, songs on records can be transferred to tape recordings and carefully interspersed with narration to make effective radio tapes. This type of work will require an operator with special technical skill.

Learning to listen. One of the greatest problems among pupils today is their inability to listen. Radios and phonographs that are turned on all day in the home have added greatly to this problem, for all ages have learned to ignore them as they go about doing other things. Christian workers must counteract this problem if records are to be used effectively in the work of the church. People must be taught to listen (these same principles apply to tape recordings). This may be done in several ways:

1. Prepare the group to listen to the record. Point out things for which to listen. Arouse their curiosity. List difficult words and ideas on the chalkboard before the record is played and talk about them.

2. Use visual aids as the record is being played. Use especially prepared charts, graphs, pictures, drawings and posters. However, do not overwork this idea. All pupils need to *learn* to listen without the aid of visuals.

3. Follow the record with a discussion or special project. A short true-false or fill-in quiz may be used to discover how well they have listened. In

Fig. 191. Portable battery-operated videotape recorder and camera (AKAI-110-S VTR)

order to provide motivation, inform the group that they will be quizzed over the materials before the record is played.

VIDEOTAPE

Inexpensive videotape recording and playback equipment represents another marvelous technological breakthrough in the late '60s and early '70s. The small portable and battery-operated units have unusual possibilities for us in Christian education (see Fig. 191):

1. They can be used to record regular meetings and services of the church as well as for evaluating purposes and leadership training.

2. They can be used to record interviews and other special activities for viewing in various class and group sessions. The equipment is such that you can take it any place outside of the regular classroom and do on-the-spot recording.

3. They can be used for videotaping relevant TV programs off the air and be played in class and small groups for discussion and interaction.

Fig. 192. Mobile VTR center

As this equipment is refined even further, and particularly with the coming of video-cassettes, the possibilities for use in Christian education learning centers and for self-study purposes is almost revolutionary (see Figs. 192-94).

Special Projects

1. Practice using the tape recorder until you can make a good quality recording without much difficulty.

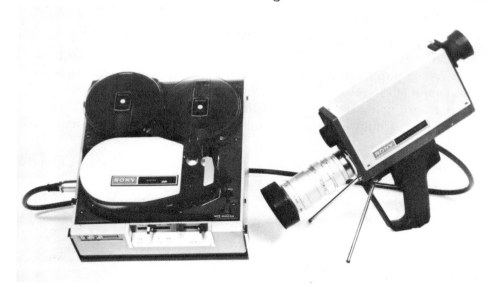

Fig. 193. Sony VTR unit

Fig. 194. Sony VTR unit

2. Be prepared to demonstrate how to splice a broken tape.

3. As a group prepare several of the following recordings:

   a. A sound recording for a filmstrip, a set of slides, a flannelboard lesson, a chalk talk, a puppet play or for an actual dramatic skit (include narration, music, sound effects, etc., if necessary for a good recording).

   b. A recording direct from the radio or a record player.

   c. A Bible or missionary story, a missionary "tape letter," a program for shut-ins, etc.

4. Practice using the tape recorder to improve individual or group verbal presentations.

5. Be prepared to demonstrate how to handle records and how to use a record player. Show how a record can actually be used in Christian education.

6. If equipment is accessible, prepare a videotape program for use in some aspect of Christian education.

13

Organizing for Audiovisuals

INTERESTING CHANGES have taken place over the last several years regarding a fundamental approach to organizing for the use of audiovisual media, particularly at the church level. When these tools first became readily available, a rather centralized plan was adopted; that is, to have one centralized audiovisual center where all hardware as well as software were stored, classified and distributed as needed.

More recently, however, a decentralized approach has become more popular. Rather than storing all equipment and materials in one place, each

Fig. 195. Mobile audiovisual equipment center (Wilson)

Fig. 196. Departmental learning center (Califone)

Fig. 197. A small class in departmental learning center (*Teach*)

department of the church has its own teaching tools. Naturally, certain expensive pieces of equipment, such as a 16 mm. projector, need to be available to all departments (see Fig. 195). But in a large church, it is advisable for each department to have its own recording equipment, overhead projector, filmstrip and slide projector, etc., as well as a file of materials designed for a particular age level or age group. This way, these materials can be used at a moment's notice, allowing teachers to make use of the spontaneous opportunities in teaching (see Figs. 196-97).

The learning center concept and an emphasis on self-study have helped to create this decentralization. A learning center is designed to include all types of media, including the traditional library materials, such as books and magazines. Along with printed materials, filmstrips, slides, recordings, and other resources are made available to students for self-study (see Figs. 198-99).

Cassette tapes have probably contributed more to this organizational approach than any other technological breakthrough. Students can listen to tapes individually or as a group, utilizing earphones. Teaching segments involving data-input can be communicated with cassettes, and then small groups or individual counseling sessions can be used to discuss the data and how it can be applied to life (see Figs 200-1).

Since the Word of God is eternal and absolute, it can be readily taught by means of cassettes. Once the basic facts of a Bible story are placed on a cassette tape, it will have timeless use. The application, of course, needs to be current and up-to-date, based on immediate cultural problems and concerns. This facet of teaching, of course, is led by individual teachers after the basic facts of the Word have been learned.

There are many advantages, of course, to personalized instruction by means of guided learning:

1. Example of biblical education, particularly in the teaching examples of Christ, are intensely personal. Thus the learning center and personalized instruction are based on a biblical philosophy of education.

2. Personalized instruction involves a process designed for each student. As someone has aptly said, this approach "is based on the idea that there is no one best teaching method for all pupils, but there are best methods to teach each pupil."

3. Personalized instruction enables students to learn at different rates. One of the problems in the average Sunday school is that we have many students who are at different levels in their knowledge and understanding of the Scripture. A learning center offering individualized self-study programs can meet the need of each student, beginning where he is in his own personal spiritual development.

Fig. 198. Using individual self-study methods (*Teach*)

Fig. 199. Individualized filmstrip viewing (Dukane)

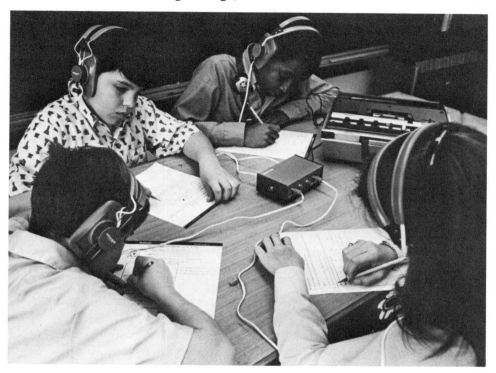

Fig. 200. Listening to a cassette tape as a group (3M)

Fig. 201. Unit for reproducing cassette tapes in quantity (Infonics)

4. This approach enables students of various ages to study in the same room but does not prohibit group meetings involving single age levels. One Christian day school has used this innovative approach to education and has all students from grade two through high school in the same room. Each student has his study carrel where he is involved in personalized learning by means of programmed materials—reading books, handouts, filmstrips, cassette tapes, etc.

5. This approach, with some careful thought, can be incorporated into a traditional program of Christian education. There are, of course, some problems with this approach, for obviously this type of program takes time to plan, organize and implement. It also takes qualified teachers. But many believe it is the approach of the future, and its advantages are such that it cannot be ignored. Modern media has made it possible, as at no other time in history, for Christians to utilize biblical principles of communication—an approach that puts an emphasis on individual learning.

Following are some specific suggestions for organizing an audiovisual program:

1. Appoint one qualified person in the church to develop a plan for audiovisual use.

2. Visit public schools and other churches that are making good use of this media. Observe their procedures and approach to organization.

3. Make sure that teachers and workers in every department of the church school have the necessary equipment and materials readily available for immediate use.

4. Conduct training classes and seminars not only in audiovisual techniques but in how to utilize audiovisuals in the light of a biblical philosophy of education that will enable them to put media in total perspective.

APPENDIX I

Using Audiovisual Media on the Mission Field

IN ORDER for audio and projected aids to be used, there needs to be a source of electrical power. In many areas of the world the missionary has an adequate source of electricity, but elsewhere there are tremendous problems because there is no electrical power.

In the majority of cities outside of the United States the voltage is 220 alternating current rather than 110 alternating current. This problem can be surmounted in the majority of cases by using a transformer; however, when motor-driven equipment is used, one must be certain that the cycles of the power supply match that for which the equipment is designed. This difficulty may be overcome in several ways. When a machine is purchased in the United States, it may be especially prepared by the manufacturer for use in a specific country. If this is not done, a special adapter kit may be obtained when the machine is purchased so that the missionary can solve the problem when he gets to the field. A special booklet may be obtained from the United States Chamber of Commerce which will give the needed information regarding voltage and cycles in all areas of the world. In places where direct current is used rather than alternating current, a synchronous converter or vibrator may be used.

In the wake of World War II, new technical knowledge brought about great changes in electronics. Transistors replaced vacuum tubes, making it possible to produce audio equipment, such as radios, tape recorders, etc., whose power requirement was but a fraction of that needed for conventional vacuum-tube models. For example, the early portable shortwave radios were supplied with a battery pack that weighed from ten to twenty-five pounds.

The new technology made it necessary for engineers to do research and improve batteries as a source of power. Today it is hard even to imagine the many types and sizes of dry-cell batteries available to power an unbelievable array of audio equipment.

It wasn't long until we began hearing about nickel cadmium cells that could be recharged and used over and over again. Today these miniature chemical laboratories are still being improved and at the same time performing a useful service in all walks of life.

Along with the improvement in electronics it was necessary to develop electric motors that could be driven by light-weight batteries and thus do away with bulky, heavy spring-driven motors. The transition was wonderful and today we have efficient motors that do the job very well.

We wish we could report dramatic advances in the field of projection. True! There have been innovations in low-voltage projection lamps, but the very best still require a power source that presents a problem in areas where adequate power is not generated.

In the late 1950s an excellent projector was available (SVE International Projector) which used a Coleman Kerosene/Gasoline Lantern (Model No. 237) as a light source. In spite of the size, heat and inconvenience, it was a functional piece of equipment. Anyone who still has one should prize it. However, the market did not warrant production so it was dropped by the manufacturer.

Several firms have tried to develop optics that would project well by using conventional flashlight batteries for power. Models now available are better than nothing at all, but there is much to be desired in this area. On the other hand, projection lamp manufacturers are producing lamps that can be powered from 6- and 12-volt power sources, making it possible to use conventional wet-cell batteries which offer adequate amperage for acceptable projection. For example, storage batteries used in automobiles, aircraft, motorcycles and other automotive vehicles have enough power to be functional. But, there must be a means for recharging such batteries! It might be of interest to those who do not know, that at one time there were home and farm lighting systems which were powered from banks of wet-cell batteries. In order to keep the batteries charged, a windmill generator was manufactured. It looked like a conventional windmill used to pump water, but instead it drove a small generator which produced enough current to keep the batteries charged. Here again, such a windmill charger would be very useful in many missionary applications. An ingenious person could very well design his own unit and make effective use of it.

Another application using wet-cell batteries involves converters (invertors). These devices change direct current into alternating current, allowing the use of audio equipment which has alternating current motors in their operation. It is important, in such uses, that the batteries have adequate amperage to accommodate the wattage required. Usually the cost involved in setting up a battery and converter unit makes it more practical to use a generator plant where the wattage requirement exceeds 100 watts.

Generators

Choosing a generator that meets your need is still important. Today there is a generator suitable for every application. However, the missionary need usually calls for one that is portable and capable of producing 1,500 to 2,000 watts. For intermittent use (once or twice a week) an alternator type power plant operating at 3,600 rpm will provide the most portable size and weight. Admittedly there is still the noise level to contend with, but this is not insurmountable.

Converters

A direct current to alternating current converter is available to permit the operation of equipment designed for alternating current from direct current lines. This direct current may come from a storage battery or any other direct current source.

Converters used with storage batteries may be used in any area where there is no electrical source. They, of course, will not do an effective job where equipment is used that eats up thousands of watts, but they are very capable for use with tape recorders, record players, small radios and projectors. How long they run before a battery needs recharging depends upon the current they draw, continuity of operation, and the size and condition of the battery.

Transformers and Voltage Regulators

Transformers are used to "step up" or "step down" voltage. For example, a transformer is needed if the source of supply is 220 alternating current or vice versa. Transformers are usually available in any area where this problem arises.

While most people are familiar with transformers, they do not realize that voltage regulators are available. This equipment is designed to meet every condition where a constant flow of current is necessary. This would apply especially when phonographs, tape recorders, and motion-picture projectors are used. Voltage regulators are available for either automatic or manual operation. This equipment is necessary where there is a change in the voltage supply.

Combating Deterioration

The efficiency of equipment in many areas depends upon how well it is cared for, particularly in the tropics. Humidity will deteriorate lenses, motors, and electrical parts. While much has been said about "tropical treatment," there is no completely satisfactory solution, but the best method at the present is to avail oneself of a weather-tight container in which equipment can be placed when it is not in use. At the same time, place the dehumidifying chemical which is readily available in most tropical areas with the equipment. Tupperware containers, home-type picnic ice chests, GI ammo boxes, and ordinary plastic bags serve as excellent containers.

Gospel Recordings

Gospel Recordings Incorporated is a worldwide missionary organization made up of a group of people who have dedicated their whole time to the making and sending out of the gospel by means of phonograph records in all languages. The number of languages and dialects in which records have been made is advancing toward the 4,000 mark. Recordists are adding new languages to the list daily as they travel from country to country.

Records are sent free of charge to those who will be responsible for using them for the purpose for which they are intended. Missionaries and Christian nationals use them and give them out wherever they can be used to spread the gospel. Gospel Recordings Incorporated does not charge for the records nor do they allow others to sell them for profit. Distributors are allowed to recover the bare amount of customs charges they have had to pay, but free distribution is encouraged wherever possible. Distribution centers are located in many countries.

Scripts, written by experienced staff members, contain simplified sermonettes, dialogues and testimonies. Scripture, Bible stories and hymns are used. Typical script titles are "Jesus Can Heal Your Soul," "The Two Roads," "Creation and Redemption," "The Crucifixion," "The Resurrection," "Behold the Lamb of God," "How God's Children Should Live," "One Mediator," and "The Only Saviour." The aim of Gospel Recordings is that each side of every record will have a clear presentation of Christ as the only Saviour and that simple teaching of Christian standards be included.

Staff recordists travel from country to country searching out languages. With the help of missionaries and Christian nationals, they find nationals of various tribal tongues who will speak or sing for recordings. With the help of interpreters, the recordist has the national translate a prepared message into his own tongue. In the case of unwritten languages and illiterate nationals, this is done carefully, using a special sentence-by-sentence recording technique. There is painstaking rechecking to safeguard the message.

Battery-operated tape recorders are used for field recording, with the tape sent back to Gospel Recordings headquarters where it is handled by special technicians who transfer the recordings to master disks. These are used in making metal negatives which in turn are used as molds or dies to press out the hundreds of records which go back to the places where they can be understood.

A small, inexpensive, unconventional phonograph—hand operated, mechanical, metal encased—will be sent out postpaid to any place in the world. They are, of course, exclusively for use on mission fields. A small motorless, continuous-wind phonette for use among primitive tribes will also be sent for a very small rate.

Three-speed, battery-powered transistorized phonographs are also available for use on the mission field. These machines are made to give good and lasting service.

Gospel Recordings has also entered the reel-to-reel and cassette field, but still find greater demands for disk recordings.

APPENDIX II

Sources of Audiovisual Materials

FLANNELBOARD MATERIALS

Child Evangelism Fellowship, P.O. Box 1156, Grand Rapids, Mich.
Gospel Light Press, 725 East Colorado, Glendale, Calif. 91205
Higley Press, Butler, Ind. 46721
Huffman Pub. Co., P.O. Box 548, Hallandale, Fla. 33009
Munn Art Studio, 306 N. West St., Hillsdale, Mich. 49242
Scripture Press, 1825 College Avenue, Wheaton, Ill. 60187
Standard Publishing Foundation, Hamilton Avenue at 8100, Cincinnati, O. 45231
Union Gospel Press, Cleveland, O. 44101
Visuals, 427 East Washington Blvd., Grove City, Pa. 16127

FLAT PICTURES

Artex Prints, Inc., Westport, Conn. 06880
Christian Board of Publication, Beaumont and Pine Blvd., Box 179, St. Louis, Mo.
Litz Services Inc., 42 Dartmouth St., Malden, Mass. 02148
Cokesbury, 1661 North Northwest Hwy., Park Ridge, Ill. 60068
National Christian Education Council, Robert Denholm House, Nutfield Red-hill, Surrey, England
Thomas Nelson and Sons, LTD., Lincoln Way Windmill Road, Sunbury-On-Thames, Middlesex, England
Sources of free and inexpensive pictures, Bruce Miller, Box 369, Riverside, Calif. 92502
Standard Publishing Foundation, Hamilton Avenue at 8100, Cincinnati, O. 45231
    Teaching pictures accompanying lesson materials of various denominations and publishers.

MATERIALS IN GENERAL

The following materials may be obtained from various religious bookstores and publishing companies:

charts	models
exhibits	objects
graphs	records
maps	

FILMS, FILMSTRIPS, AND SLIDES

Association Films, 600 Madison, New York, N.Y. 10022

Bailey Films, 6509 Delongpre Ave., Hollywood 23, Calif.

Baptista Films, Sunnyside Avenue, Wheaton, Ill.

Berean Gospel Distributors, Inc., P.O. Box 891, Indianapolis 6, Ind.

Broadman Productions, 161-8th Avenue North, Nashville 3, Tenn.

Cathedral Films, 2921 W. Alemeda Ave., Burbank, Calif.

Church Film Service, 2595 Manderson Street, Omaha 11, Nebr.

Cokesbury, Curriculum A-V Dept., 201 8th Ave. South, Nashville, Tenn. 37203

Concordia Audio-Visual Service, 3558 S. Jefferson St., St. Louis, Mo. 63118

Evangelical Communications Research Foundation, Box 28539, Dallas, Tex. 75228

Family Films, Inc., 5823 Santa Monica Blvd., Hollywood, Calif.

Gospel Films Inc., Box 455, Muskegon, Mich.

Gospel Light, 725 East Colorado, Glendale, Calif. 91205

Inter-Varsity, 2330 Langdon St., Madison, Wisc. 53703

Ken Anderson, Inc., Box 618, Winona Lake, Ind.

Life Film Strips, Time-Life Building, Rockefeller Center, New York, N.Y. 10020

Moody Bible Institute Film Department, 820 N. LaSalle St., Chicago, Ill. 60610

Moody Institute of Science, 12000 E. Washington Blvd., Whittier, Calif.

National Education Association, 1201-16th St., Northwest, Washington, D.C. 20036

Scripture Press, 1825 College Ave., Wheaton, Ill.

Society for Visual Education, Inc., 1345 Diversey Parkway, Chicago, Ill. 60614

Space Age Communications—Educational, Box 11008, Dallas, Tex. 75223.

Tabernacle Pictures, 923 S. Eye Street, Tacoma 3, Wash.

Univeristy of Michigan Audio-Visual Dept., Frieze Bldg., 720 E. Huron, Ann Arbor, Mich. 48104

Unusual Films, Bob Jones University, Greenville, S.C.

Youth For Christ International, Film Department, 109 N. Cross Street, Wheaton, Ill.

OBJECT-LESSON BOOKS

Clark, Ruth. *Object Talks for Special Occasions.* Cincinnati, O.: Standard.

DeGolia, J. E. *Object Lessons.* Wheaton, Ill.: Scripture Press.

Doan, Eleanor. *Fascinating Finger Fun.* Grand Rapids: Zondervan.

Foushee, Clyde. *Animated Object Talks.* Los Angeles: Revell.

————. *52 Workable Youth Object Lessons.* Grand Rapids: Zondervan.

———. *Object Lessons for Youth*. Grand Rapids: Zondervan.
Hoy, David. *Magic with a Message*. Westwood, N.J.: Revell.
McLean, W. T. *Illustrated Gospel Object Lessons*. Grand Rapids: Zondervan.
Miller, Basil. *Chemical Illustrations*. Grand Rapids: Zondervan.
———. *20 Illustrated Object Lessons*. Grand Rapids: Zondervan.
Pentecost, Dorothy. *Simple Object Lessons for Special Days and Occasions*. Grand
  Rapids: Zondervan.
Ryrie, Charles C. *Easy-to-Get-Object Lessons*. Grand Rapids: Zondervan.
———. *Object Lessons Easy to Give*. Grand Rapids: Zondervan.
———. *Object Lessons Quick to See*. Grand Rapids: Zondervan.
Talbot, Louis T. *Objects That Talk and Teach*. Grand Rapids: Zondervan.
———. *More Objects That Talk and Teach*. Grand Rapids: Zondervan.
———. *Still More Object Lessons That Talk and Teach*. Grand Rapids: Zondervan.
Thompson, David W. *Bible Magic Rule Object Lessons*. Cincinnati: Standard.
Westphal, Arnold. *Westphal's Simple Surprise Object Lessons*. Grand Rapids:
  Zondervan.
———. *Westphal's Visual Surprise Object Lessons*. Grand Rapids: Zondervan.
Wilder, Elmer L. *Easy Object Lessons*. Grand Rapids: Zondervan.
———. *Heart Reaching Object Lessons*. Grand Rapids: Zondervan.
———. *Object Lessons for Boys and Girls*. Grand Rapids: Zondervan.
———. *Talking Visuals*. Los Angeles: Bible House of Los Angeles.
———. *See It! Object Lessons*. Grand Rapids: Zondervan.
———. *Talking Object Lessons*. Grand Rapids: Zondervan.
———. *Talking Visuals*. Grand Rapids: Kregel.

BOOKS ON CHALK TALKS

Barnett, Stella O. *How to Make Chalk Talk*. Westwood, N.J.: Revell.
Bixler, William A. *Chalk Talk Made Easy*. Anderson, Ind.: Warner.
Hunt, Lionel A. *Chalk Talks for the Amateur*. Chicago: Moody.
Sweeting, George. *How to Be a Chalk Artist*. Grand Rapids: Zondervan.

RECORDS

Audio Bible Studies, 5574 E. Washington Blvd., Los Angeles 22, Calif. (Chicago
  office—231 W. Chicago Ave., Chicago, Ill.)
Gospel Light, 725 East Colorado, Glendale, Calif. 91205
Word Records, Inc., Box 1790, Waco, Tex.

APPENDIX III

Sources of Audiovisual Equipment

Bulletin Boards and Chalkboards

Acme Bulletin Co., 37 East 12th St., New York, N.Y. 10003
Bulletin Boards and Directory Products, 724 Broadway, New York, N.Y. 10003
Christian Publications, Inc., 25 S. 10th St., Harrisburg, Pa. 17101
Endur Products Co., 407 Goshen Ave., Visalia, Calif.
Redikut Letter Co., 12617 South Prairie Ave., Hawthorne, Calif. 90250
Litz Bureau Div., Remington Rand Office Systems Division, 801 Park Ave., Herkimer, N.Y. 13350

Camera Equipment

Ansco, 40 Charles St., Binghamton, N.Y.
Argus Cameras, Inc., 405 Fourth St., Ann Arbor, Mich.
Eastman Kodak Co., Rochester, N.Y.
Exakta Camera Co., 705 Bronx River Road, Bronxville, N.Y. 10708
Polaroid Corp., Cambridge, Mass.

Filmstrip and Slide Projectors

Bell and Howell Co., A-V Products Division, 7100 McCormick Road, Chicago, Ill. 60645
Dukane Corp., St. Charles, Ill. 60174
Mighty Mite, Mitchel Art Productions, P.O. Box 25005, W. Los Angeles, Calif.
Graflex Co., Div. of the Singer Corp., 3759 Monroe Ave., Rochester, N.Y. 14603
Society for Visual Education, Inc., 1345 West Diversey Parkway, Chicago, Ill. 60614
Viewlex, Inc., Holbrook, N.Y. 11741

SOUND MOTION-PICTURE PROJECTORS

Ampro Corporation, 2835 N. Western Ave., Chicago, Ill. 60618

Bell and Howell Co., A-V Products Division, 7100 McCormick Road, Chicago, Ill. 60645

Comprehensive Service Corp., 245 West 55th St., New York, N.Y.

Graflex Co., Division of the Singer Co., 3759 Monroe Ave., Rochester, N.Y. 14603

Eastman Kodak Co., 343 State St., Rochester, N.Y.

Harwald Co., Inc., 1216 Chicago Ave., Evanston, Ill.

Holmes Projector Co., 1815 Orchard St., Chicago, Ill. 60614

Technical Service, Inc., 30865 Five Mile Road, Livonia, Mich.

Victor Animatograph Corp., Plainville, Conn.

OVERHEAD OPAQUE PROJECTORS

Buhl Projector Co., Inc., 1770 New Highway, Farmingdale, N.Y. 11735

Don Howell, Audio-Visual Products Division, 7100 McCormick Road, Chicago, Ill. 60645

Graflex, Inc., 3750 Monroe Ave., Rochester, N.Y. 14603

H. Wilson Corp., 55 West 166th St., South Holland, Ill. 60473

Minnesota Mining and Manufacturing Co., 2501 Hudson Road, St. Paul, Minn. 55119

Projection Optics, Co., Inc., 271 11th Ave., East Orange, N.J. 07018

RECORD PLAYERS

Audiotronics Corp., 7428 Belaire Ave., Box 151, North Hollywood, Calif.

Magnavox Co., Fort Wayne, Ind.

Radio Corporation of America, Inc., Front and Cooper Sts., Camden, N.J. 08102

PROJECTION SCREENS

Da-Lite Screen Co., Inc., State Road #15, North, Warsaw, Ind. 46580

Lightmaster Screen Co., 12270 Montague St., Building 57, Pacoima, Calif.

Radiant Manufacturing Corp., 8220 N. Austin Ave., Morton Grove, Ill. 60053

Raven Screen Corp., 124 East 124th St., New York ,N.Y. 10035

TAPE RECORDERS

Ampex Corp., 2201 Lunt Ave., Elk Grove Village, Ill. 60007

Audiotronics Corp., 7428 Belaire Ave., Box 151, North Hollywood, Calif.

Bell and Howell Co., A-V Products Div., 7100 McCormick Road, Chicago, Ill. 60645

Concord Electronics, 1935 Armacost Ave., Los Angeles, Calif. 90025

Radio Corporation of America, Front and Cooper Sts., Camden, N.J.

Sony Corporation of America, 5551 North Milton Parkway, Rosemont, Ill. 60018

Webcor, Inc., 5610 Bloomingdale Ave., Chicago 39, Ill.

Webster Electric Co., 1900 Clark St., Racine, Wisc. 53403

APPENDIX IV

Sources of Films and Filmstrips for Teaching a Course in Audiovisual Media

SOUND FILMS

Accent on Learning (Ohio State University)
Audio-Visual Materials in Teaching (Coronet Films)
Better Bulletin Boards (Indiana University)
Bulletin Boards: An Effective Teaching Device (Bailey Films)
Chalk and Chalkboards (Bailey Films)
Chalkboard Utilization (University of Wisconsin)
Dry Mount for Teaching Pictures (Syracuse University)
Dry Mounting (McGraw-Hill)
Facts About Film (International Film Bureau)
Facts About Projection (International Film Bureau)
Feltboard in Teaching (Wayne University)
Felt Pen Sketching (Young American Films)
Field Trip (Virginia Education Board)
Flannelboards and How to Use Them (Bailey Films)
Flannelgraph—Its Application (University of Minnesota)
Globes: Their Function in the Classroom (Bailey Films)
Hand-Made Materials for Projection (Indiana University)
How to Make and Use Dioramas (McGraw-Hill)
Learning to Draw (Capital Film Service)
Lettering Instruction Materials (Indiana University)
Magazines to Transparencies (Florida State University)
Mural Making (International Film Bureau)

Opaque Projector—Its Purpose and Use (University of Iowa)
Operation and Care of Bell & Howell Sound Projector (International Film Bureau)
Operation and Care of RCA 400 Sound Projector (International Film Bureau)
Operation and Care of the Ampro Projector (International Film Bureau)
Operation and Care of Victor Sound Projector (International Film Bureau)
Photographic Slides for Instruction (Indiana University)
Poster Making: Design and Technique (Bailey Films)
Poster Making: Printing by Silk Screen (Bailey Films)
Projecting Motion Pictures (University of California)
Recording with Magnetic Tape (University of Minnesota)
Tape Recording for Instruction (Indiana University)
The Unique Contribution (Encyclopedia Brittanica)
Using Visuals in Your Speech (McGraw-Hill)
Wet Mounting Pictorial Materials (Indiana University)

FILM STRIPS

Beyond the Textbook (Visual Education Service)
Bulletin Boards at Work (Wayne University)
Enriching the Curriculum with Filmstrips (Society for Visual Education)
How-To for Church School Teachers (Concordia Films)
How to Keep Bulletin Boards Alive (Ohio State University)
How to Organize for Audio-Visuals in Your Church (Family Films)
How to Make and Use the Feltboard (Ohio State University)
How to Use a Filmstrip (Eye-Gate House)
How to Use Filmstrips in Your Church (Family Filmstrips)
How to Use Motion Pictures in Your Church (Family Filmstrips)
Improving the Use of the Chalkboard (Ohio State University)
Making Field Trips Effective (Wayne University)
The Opaque Projector (Ohio State University)
Our Audiovisual Heritage (Society for Visual Education)
A Parade of Bulletin Boards (Ohio State University)
Phil M. Strip (United Church of Canada)
A Simple Exhibit Technique (Ohio State University)
Simplified Filmstrip Production (Ohio State University)
Teaching with Still Pictures (Basic Skills Films)
Tips on Slide Films (Jam Handy)
Training Kit for Using Audio-Visuals in the Church (Family Films)
Why Use Audio-Visuals in Your Church (Family Filmstrips)

Notes

CHAPTER 1

1. William T. Harris, *International Education Series* (New York: Appleton, 1898), p. 120.
2. John A. Comenius, *The Great Didactic*, trans. M. W. Keatings (London: Black, 1896), pp. 291-92.
3. Ellwood P. Cubberley, *The History of Education* (New York: Houghton Mifflin, 1948), p. 410.
4. Comenius, p. 291.

CHAPTER 2

1. Edgar Dale, *Audio-Visual Methods in Teaching* (New York: Dryden, 1954), p. 30.
2. Dale, "The Why of Audio-Visual Materials," *The Audio-Visual Reader*, ed. J. S. Kinder and F. D. McClusky (Dubuque: Brown, 1954), p. 1.
3. "Good Humor," *The Sudan Witness*, Nov.-Dec. 1956, p. 6.
4. F. D. McClusky, "Values in Audio-Visual Instruction," *The Audio-Visual Reader*, p. 8.
5. Dale, "The Why of Audio-Visual Materials," p. 2.
6. Daniel R. Martin, "More to Be Taught to More" *Educational Resources and Techniques*, Sept. 1961, p. 4.
7. *A Teacher's Guide to Overhead Projection* (Holyoke, Mass.: Technifax Corp., 1959), p. 9.
8. Dale, *Audiovisual Methods of Teaching*, rev. ed. (New York: Holt, Rinehart & Winston, 1954), p. 65.

CHAPTER 3

1. Francis A. Schaeffer, *The Church at the End of the 20th Century* (Downers Grove, Ill.: Inter-Varsity, 1970), p. 77.

CHAPTER 6

1. Marjorie East, *Display for Learning* (New York: Dryden, 1952), p. 42.

CHAPTER 7

1. Two weeks may be spent on each department, featuring the superintendent, the teachers, class officers and other interesting facts, such as attendance, growth, etc.
2. Figures 72-77 are reprinted from *Flannelgraph Helps* by Gladys Siegfried and used by permission of Scripture Press, Wheaton, Ill., publisher of many excellent flannelgraph materials.

CHAPTER 8

1. Robert DeKieffer and Lee W. Cochran, *Manual of Audio-Visual Techniques* (Englewood Cliffs, N.J.: Prentice-Hall, 1955), p. 19.
2. Lois LeBar, *Children in the Bible School* (Westwood, N.J.: Revell, 1952), p. 270.
3. Marjorie East, *Display for Learning* (New York: Dryden, 1952), p. 74.
4. Minnesota Mining and Manufacturing Co., St. Paul, Minn.
5. Most audiovisual specialists include the subject of "posters" in the category of "graphic materials." However, it is included here since many of the posters used in the area of Christian education are of a pictorial nature.
6. See Appendix IV.

CHAPTER 9

1. Richard E. Smith. *The Overhead System* (Austin: U. Texas), p. 9.
2. A small, light-weight projector with a light source in the head was introduced by the 3M Company in 1965. However, this projector has serious limitations and is recommended for small groups only.
3. Herbert E. Scuorzo, *The Practical Audio-Visual Handbook for Teachers*. (West Nyack, N.Y.: Parker, 1967), p. 45.
4. These most common types of transparencies are outlined in this chapter: handmade, heat-transfer and diazo. However, several others warrant your attention, including photographic ("wet process") transparencies, and color-lift transparencies. For thorough instructions for making these visuals see Smith, pp. 41-44, 56-61.
5. Smith, pp. 64-65.
6. Duane Litfin, "Bible Teaching with the Overhead Projector" (Master's thesis, Dallas Theological Seminary, 1970), pp. 68-70.
7. Emil W. Grieshaber, "Overhead Projection," *Audio-Visual Instruction*, April 1962, p. 237.
8. Richard P. Weagley, *Teaching with the Overhead Projector* (Philadelphia: Instructo Products Co., 1963), p. 31.
9. Ibid., p. 30.
10. Grieshaber, p. 237.
11. Morton J. Shultz, *The Teacher and Overhead Projection* (Englewood Cliffs, N.J.: Prentice-Hall, 1965), p. 11.
12. Herbert E. Scuorzo, *The Practical Audio-Visual Handbook for Teachers* (West Nyack, N.Y.: Parker, 1967), p. 68.
13. Grieshaber, p. 237.

CHAPTER 10

1. The specific film and the occasion determine the amount of time spent in preparing the group for the film, and in application.
2. For further helps in discovering how to solve projection problems, see *The Audio-Visual Projectionist Handbook* (Chicago: Business Screen Magazines, 1953).
3. Glen Arnold, "How to Produce a Children's Film Without Actually Crying," *Moody Monthly*, Apr. 1971, p. 131.

CHAPTER 11

1. See Charles A. Kinsley. "Bad Weather Pictures," *Here's How* (Rochester, N.Y.: Eastman Kodak, 1967), pp. 10-17.
2. Don Nibbelink, "Subject Control for Better Pictures," *Here's How*, pp. 20-24.

CHAPTER 12

1. See Appendix IV.

Bibliography

BOOKS

Babin, Pierre. *The Audio-Visual Man.* Dayton, O.: Pflaum, 1970.

Bachman, John W. *How to Use Audio-Visual Materials.* New York: Association Press, 1956. Pp. 60.

Brown, James W. and Lewis, Richard B. eds. *A.V. Instructional Materials Manual.* San Jose: Spartan Book Store, 1957. Pp. 191.

Cassell, Sylvia. *Fun with Puppets.* Nashville: Broadman, 1956. Pp. 113.

Dale, Edgar. *Audio-Visual Methods in Teaching,* new ed. New York: Dryden, 1954. Pp. 534.

DeKieffer, Robert and Cochran, Lee W. *Manual of Audio-Visual Techniques.* Englewood Cliffs, N.J.: Prentice-Hall, 1955. Pp. 219.

East, Marjorie. *Display for Learning.* New York: Dryden, 1952. Pp. 306.

Eboch, Sidney C. *Operating Audio-Visual Equipment.* San Francisco: Chandler, 1968. Pp. 76.

Erickson, Carlton, W. H. *Fundamentals of Teaching with Audio-Visual Technology.* New York: Macmillan, 1965. Pp. 384.

Finn, James D. *The Audio-Visual Equipment Manual.* New York: Dryden, 1957. Pp. 363.

Flannelgraph Helps. Chicago: Scripture Press. Pp. 23.

Guimarin, Spencer. *Lettering Techniques.* Austin, Tex.: Visual Instruction Bureau, Division of Extension, U. Texas, 1965. Pp. 50.

Jackson, B. F., ed. *Communication—Learning for Churchmen.* Nashville: Abingdon, 1968. Pp. 297.

Kemp, Jerrold E. *Planning and Producing Audiovisual Materials.* San Francisco: Chandler, 1963. Pp. 251.

Linker, Jerry Mac. *Designing Instructional Visuals.* Austin, Tex.: Visual Instruction Bureau, Division of Extension, U. Texas, 1968. Pp. 35.

Sands, Lester B. *Audio-Visual Procedures in Teaching.* New York: Ronald, 1956. Pp. 670.

231

Scuorzo, Herbert E. *Practical Audiovisual Handbook for Teachers.* West Nyack, N.Y.: Parker, 1967. Pp. 211.

Smith, Richard E. *The Overhead System.* Austin, Tex.: Visual Instruction Bureau, Division of Extension, U. Texas, n.d. Pp. 107.

Tower, Howard E. *Church Use of Audio-Visuals.* New York: Abingdon, 1950. Pp. 152.

Using Audio-Visuals in the Church. Chicago: The National Council of Churches of Christ in the United States of America, 1950. Pp. 16.

Waldrup, Earl. *Using Visual Aids in a Church.* Nashville: Broadman, 1949. Pp. 178.

Magazines and Periodicals

Baptist Leader, Baptist Board of Education and Publication, Valley Forge, Pa. 19481.

Christian Life, Schmale Road and Gunderson Dr., Wheaton, Ill. 60187 (Film reviews).

Educational Media, 1015 Florence St., Fort Worth, Tex.

Educational Technology, 140 Sylvan Ave., Englewood Cliffs, N.J. 07632.

Helps for the Month, Church-Craft Pictures, St. Louis, Mo.

Key to Christian Education, Standard Publishing Co., 8121 Hamilton Ave., Cincinnati, O. 45231.

Outreach, Southern Baptist Convention, 127 9th Ave. North, Nashville, Tenn. 37203.

Resource, 2900 Queen Lane, Philadelphia, Pa. 19129.

Sunday School Counselor, Assemblies of God, 1445 Boonville, Springfield, Mo. 65802.

Teach, Gospel Light Publications, 725 East Colorado, Glendale, Calif. 91205.

Index